DECISION

Books by Richard Harris

THE REAL VOICE
A SACRED TRUST
THE FEAR OF CRIME
JUSTICE
DECISION

DECISION

by Richard Harris

E. P. DUTTON & CO., INC. | NEW YORK | 1971

Published simultaneously in Canada by Clarke, Irwin & Company Limited,
Toronto and Vancouver

Library of Congress Catalog Card Number: 77-148469

Most of the contents of this book appeared originally in
The New Yorker, in somewhat different form.

SBN: 0-525-08955-1

ACKNOWLEDGMENT

Many people provided information for this book, but since some of them prefer to remain anonymous and it would slight their part to mention only the others, I would like to thank all of them for their help. Of those who assisted me editorially, I particularly want to thank Robert Bingham, of *The New Yorker*, for his care and spirit in working with me on this project and others over the years, and Hal Scharlatt, of E. P. Dutton, for his consideration and support.

On the morning of February 25, 1970, Dr. Aaron Henry, a Negro and the head of the N.A.A.C.P. in Mississippi, appeared before the Senate Subcommittee on Constitutional Rights to urge that the Voting Rights Act of 1965, which was due to expire in a few months, be renewed for at least another five years. The law was one of the most effective pieces of civil-rights legislation on the books; it had enfranchised nearly a million Negroes in the Deep South and had led to the election of about five hundred black officials there in less than five years. Civil-rights supporters had been working frantically to renew the act, while members of the Nixon Administration had been working just as frantically to revise and, it appeared, gut it.

Dr. Henry did not mention that there had been repeated attempts to murder him or that his home had been bombed and burned in retaliation for his work on behalf of Negro equality. But he did speak of what had happened to many other blacks, and a few whites, in the South. "Some of you remember . . . Dippy Smith, a friend of mine who was killed on the courthouse lawn in Brookhaven, Mississippi, as he attempted to participate in the election process," he told the subcommittee.

"George Lee was shot down in Belzoni because he would not take his name off the books. None of you can forget January, 1965—at least, I never can—the last time the poll taxes were required as a prerequisite to voting in my home state prior to the passage of this act, and Vernon Dahmer, loyal friend and worker, decided that to be of assistance, because so many people were afraid to carry their poll tax to the sheriff in Forrest County, that he would collect it himself and pay it. This was his crime, and as a result . . . Vernon's house was fire-bombed, shot into. He died a martyr, trying to make sure that the democracy that we so proudly expound in our country becomes a reality. Certainly I knew all of these men personally and appear before you today in turn that they shall not have died in vain. While the death of these men is directly attributed to their action of voting, many more, some black, some white—Whorlist Jackson, James Chaney, Andrew Goodman, Michael Schwerner—all met death because their activity was devoted to voting rights as well as other general desegregation activity in my home state. And you see, when you have to live with the truth, Andrew Goodman, a young Jewish boy from New York City, a student at Queens College, came to Mississippi at my invitation. I brought him from his mama's house to my house, and the only night that Andrew spent alive in Mississippi was in my bed. We sent him to Meridian the next day, and, of course, they went on over to Philadelphia, where the church had been burned. Coming back home that night, they were arrested, and his mama never saw him alive again."

At the end of Dr. Henry's testimony, Senator Birch Bayh, Democrat of Indiana, who was serving as the acting chairman of the subcommittee that morning, told him, "I have heard a great deal of testimony in the period I have been in the Senate. I never heard any that I felt exceeded yours in its compassionate sincerity."

8

When the session concluded, a few minutes later, Senator Bayh and one of his aides left the hearing chamber, on the second floor of the New Senate Office Building, and headed for the elevator and thence the tunnel leading to the Old Senate Office Building across the street where Bayh's suite of offices was. The Senator was still moved by what he had heard, and on the way he kept talking about the quiet bravery of men like Dr. Henry and about how the Administration's attempt to wreck the Voting Rights Act was one more piece of evidence—if any more was needed—that the President was pursuing a "Southern strategy." Finally, as Bayh reached the door to his office, he paused for a moment and muttered, "How can you listen to these stories and then let Carswell go on the Court?"

Of all the actions that President Richard Nixon took during his first two years in office, probably none more clearly revealed the character of his Presidency—the regional and class appeals that divided the nation, the disregard for the Constitutional separation of powers, the embittered relations between the Administration and the Senate, the apparent confidence that the people would sleep through even the noisiest raid on their liberties, and the belief that members of Congress could be counted on to put their own political interest above the public interest—than his nomination of George Harrold Carswell, of Florida, to be an associate justice of the Supreme Court.

Like many other senators, Bayh had become increasingly troubled, over the five weeks since the nomination had been sent to the Senate, by a growing awareness of what it meant to the country. Most of all, he was now convinced that the President's choice constituted final proof that the Administration was indeed pursuing a Southern strategy. The threat that this policy—affronting millions of black citizens—posed to the nation seemed obvious to Bayh. Far less obvious was what could be done about it. No one wanted to go through another

prolonged and politically bruising battle like the one following Judge Clement F. Haynsworth's nomination to the Court
six months before, and the mood of the Senate after that was
overwhelmingly to accept whatever name Mr. Nixon sent
over next. In the view of some senators, the President's second choice was actually an attempt to get the kind of man on
the Court he had wanted all along but had feared the Senate
would not accept the first time around—that is, someone who
would clearly demonstrate that the Administration meant to
keep the promises Mr. Nixon had made in the South during
the campaign in 1968.

It was reported that Attorney General John N. Mitchell
had gone over Carswell's record personally and afterward had
said, "He's almost too good to be true." It was not reported
what he meant by "good," but most Negro leaders assumed
that what was good for Mitchell would probably be bad
for them and their followers. William Raspberry, a Negro
columnist on the Washington *Post*, pointed out that the test
of a Supreme Court nominee was whether he was "committed
to even-handed justice," and he added, "That is the test that
Carswell, on his record, cannot meet. And his failure to meet
it is the chief reason he has been nominated."

In the view of one leading Republican who finally cast a
crucial vote against Carswell, the choice was also an attempt
to rub the Senate's nose in the mess it had made of the Haynsworth nomination. "I learned that the Justice Department had
rated Carswell way down below Haynsworth and a couple
of other candidates," this senator said later. "That made it clear
that the choice of Carswell was vengeance—to make us sorry
we hadn't accepted Haynsworth—and, at the same time, it was
an attempt to downgrade the Supreme Court and implement
the Southern strategy. The Attorney General obviously be-

lieved that we had no stomach for another fight after Haynsworth, and that we would accept any dog, so he took this
opportunity to show his disdain for the Senate. He and a lot
of the other fellows downtown seem to feel that they, and they
alone, constitute the government of the United States."

If that was the case, the President's move was a gross vio-
lation of the Constitutional rule that the three branches of
government must be separate and equal. While that precept
is repeatedly ignored in small ways during the day-to-day
operations of the government, it has rarely been so flagrantly
violated by a President—in fact, probably not since Franklin
Roosevelt tried to pack the Court a generation ago. In effect,
Mr. Nixon's move meant that he was prepared to insult one
branch of the government, the Senate, in order to lower the
quality and lessen the integrity of a second branch, the Judiciary as symbolized by the Supreme Court, in order to give
unequal power to the Executive—all for the purpose of better-
ing his own prospects for reëlection.

In any event, Senator Bayh, who had led the fight to block
Haynsworth, had little desire for an active role in another
struggle like it, and even less for the task of actually leading
it. "When a bad thing is before the Senate and it has the
support of the President, any effort to defeat it has to be
immense to succeed," he explained not long ago. "At the time,
there seemed no chance that an effort of that magnitude could
be pulled off—even though the Carswell nomination was
clearly bad—because the senators' mood was 'God, don't put
us through that again!' Also, there were other things for me
to consider. One was that I had spent eight years here trying to
build an image of myself as someone who isn't devisive, who
isn't vindictive, who can get along with all factions. If I took
on Carswell after having taken on Haynsworth, that could

all vanish, because a lot of people would figure I was just out for blood."

Despite these reservations, Bayh, along with a couple of other senators, had already gone to considerable lengths at least to keep the door open for an all-out campaign against Carswell, but so far they had concentrated largely on delaying tactics, and neither Bayh nor anyone else in the Senate was prepared at that time to come out into the open and actively lead such a campaign. That morning, though, the testimony at the hearing—and, perhaps even more important, the inevitable comparison of his own courage with that of Dr. Henry, who had fought the same fight not twice but hundreds of times, and not at the risk of his reputation but of his life— pushed Bayh closer to a decision.

That afternoon, Bayh happened to be in the Senate chamber when Senator Edward W. Brooke, Republican of Massachusetts, and the only Negro member of the Senate, took the floor and said, "I will vote against confirmation of Judge Carswell." Only a handful of other senators were present—Charles E. Goodell, of New York, who had been the first Republican to announce his opposition to Carswell, three weeks earlier; Edward M. Kennedy, of Massachusetts, the Majority Whip, who was also opposed; and Republicans Mark O. Hatfield, of Oregon, Charles H. Percy, of Illinois, Charles McC. Mathias, of Maryland, and Robert P. Griffin, of Michigan, the Minority Whip, all of whom were known or believed to support the nomination—and each man listened intently as Brooke proceeded to defend his position. Everyone there knew that it was an important occasion, because Brooke, though a rather retiring man for a politician, was an adroit leader when he decided that the time and the issue were right for him to make a move. And, of course, everyone there knew that he had rounded up many of the seventeen Republican votes that were cast against Haynsworth.

Brooke had delayed for five weeks before coming out against

14

Carswell, and that delay angered, and still angers, some liberals who felt that the case against the nomination had been compellingly clear at least three weeks earlier, and that those three weeks would have been crucial had it not been for a number of fortuitous breaks on their side, which he could not have foreseen at the time. But it appeared that Brooke had not made up his mind to act until he was sure of two things: first, that the evidence against Carswell was strong enough to justify a determined attempt to defeat him, and not just the kind of standard political grandstanding that many senators engage in under such circumstances; and, second, that there was a fair chance that an impressive number of senators, at least a third of them, could be rounded up to show the black and the young people in the country that their demands were understood. Without such support, it was said, Brooke felt that he could not oppose a President of his own party twice in a row on a Supreme Court nomination without losing whatever influence he had with the White House.

Brooke's argument against Carswell that day was based on matters that had come to light about the Judge since he was nominated, on January 19th. The first of these was a speech that he made, on August 2, 1948, before a meeting of the American Legion while he was campaigning for a seat in the Georgia legislature. In that speech, Carswell said, "I am a Southerner by ancestry, birth, training, inclination, belief, and practice. I believe that segregation of the races is proper and the only practical and correct way of life in our states. I have always so believed, and I shall always so act. I shall be the last to submit to any attempt on the part of anyone to break down and to weaken this firmly established policy of our people. . . . I yield to no man as a fellow-

15

candidate, or as a fellow-citizen, in the firm, vigorous belief in the principles of white supremacy, and I shall always be so governed." Immediately after the speech was turned up, two days after his nomination, Carswell went on television and said, "Specifically and categorically, I denounce and reject the words themselves and the ideas they represent. They're obnoxious and abhorrent to my personal philosophy." Carswell also explained that the speech had been made in the heat of a political campaign, that he had been only twenty-eight years old at the time, and that he had actually been the more liberal candidate in the race, which he had lost because of that.

In the hearings on his nomination conducted by the Senate Judiciary Committee for five days at the end of January and the beginning of February, Carswell repeated his repudiation of the 1948 speech. Senator Philip A. Hart, Democrat of Michigan, who was perhaps the committee's gentlest and also most incisive cross-examiner, then asked Carswell whether he had believed what he said at the time. Of course, that was like asking the Judge to choose between saying he had once been a liar and saying he had once been a racist. "I suppose I believed it," Carswell replied, and went on to say that it was entirely alien to his present way of thinking. To get a better idea of what that thinking was, Senator Kennedy asked him for a general exposition of what he saw as the major problems confronting the country, and Carswell listed those that came to mind—poverty, drug addiction, crime, and "the frustrations of many young people." He said nothing about race or civil rights.

Senator Brooke did not find Carswell's explanation of the reasons for his speech at all convincing. "I tried to put myself in the position of this man as best I could, under the circumstances prevailing at that time, to see if these were just political words or whether they went deeper," he told his fellow-senators. "I found that they were deeply felt words. Then I examined the age of the nominee at the time the statement was made. He was twenty-eight years of age. At that age, I had spent five years in war. In many respects, Judge Carswell and I were passing through a similar period, since we were both coming out of military service and had both gone to law school at the same time. I think I was pretty much a man at twenty-eight years of age." Going on to observe that a man could change, Brooke added, "I searched the record looking for that change. But I must confess, regrettably, that I did not find any. In fact, I found considerable evidence to the contrary. I found that in periods along the way in Judge Carswell's public career he had made statements and had acted and conducted his court in a manner which indicated to me that there was no change, that he still harbored racist views. Then I thought about our country. Where is our country going today? Many things that have been happening in this country recently, including the statements of some of our highest political leaders, made me think: Are we really moving, as the Kerner Commission report suggested, toward two societies, one black and one white? Do we really want war between the races of this nation? Did President Nixon really mean it when he said he would bring us together?"

At this point, Bayh rose and asked for the floor. Brooke yielded it at once, and Bayh talked for a few moments about the problem of convincing the disenfranchised and the discontented that there was hope for them within the system, about the grave danger of violence erupting throughout the country if they were not convinced, and then said, "The thing that concerns me is how are these people going to look at the system if they know that a man who unfortunately has this background is sitting at the very top of it?"

Brooke nodded and replied, "I do not think this nation can afford G. Harrold Carswell on the Supreme Court."

On the question of Carswell's civil-rights record, Brooke cited a number of episodes to show that Carswell had by no means abandoned the racial views he had expressed twenty-two years before. Among these was that in 1953, while Carswell was engaged in private law practice in Tallahassee, he drew up the incorporation papers for a white-only fraternity known as the Seminole Boosters, of which he was a principal subscriber and a charter member. Then, in 1956, while he was serving as United States Attorney in Florida, he helped incorporate a Tallahassee golf course that was being trans-ferred, on a ninety-nine-year lease at a dollar a year, from a public, city-owned facility, which had been built with thirty-five thousand dollars of federal money, to a private club—a move that was clearly made to circumvent a Supreme Court decision handed down about six months before prohibiting segregation in municipal recreation facilities.

In the hearings, Judge Carswell repeatedly denied having been told that this was why the public course was made private. "I consider Judge Carswell's testimony on this epi-sode disingenuous," Brooke said. "I cannot believe that he was unaware that the scheme had a discriminatory purpose transparently at odds with then current rulings of the Su-preme Court. Indeed, affidavits from black and white citizens of Tallahassee attest to the fact that the private country-club arrangements were commonly known to be a ruse to evade compliance with the Court's standards. Least of all is it likely that a U.S. Attorney, familiar with developing federal law in this field, could have been oblivious to the implications of this maneuver. Most serious is the indication that Mr. Carswell, who had sworn to uphold the Constitution and the laws of the land, would have lent his support to such an effort. What might be discounted, though not condoned, on the part of some private citizens is a grave breach of responsibility on the part of a federal official responsible for enforcing the guarantees of equal protection of the law to all citizens. It does nothing to remove the lingering suspicion that he continued to adhere to his 1948 views."

Brooke went on to point out that as a judge Carswell had an extraordinarily poor record in habeas-corpus petitions, which he had repeatedly turned down without so much as holding hearings, and that on the bench he had been demonstrably and continually antagonistic to civil-rights lawyers for no apparent reason other than that they were civil-rights lawyers. In evaluating the Judge's attitude toward school desegregation, Brooke said that he "consistently moved at the slowest possible pace, repeatedly stretching out judicial action and effectively delaying relief for those seeking reasonable compliance with the historic requirements of the 1954 Brown [v. Board of Education] decision." Brooke then asked the small group of senators who were present in the chamber, "Is it really suggestive of a commitment to equal opportunity that Judge Carswell consistently approved desegregation plans that would have postponed compliance until the mid-seventies, two decades after the Court decreed that school boards should act with all deliberate speed?"

Although it was unusual for a senator of Brooke's standing to oppose his President on an issue of this magnitude when only a handful of senators from either party had taken that position (he was the eighteenth member of the Senate to announce his opposition to Carswell, and the second Republican), the speech got little attention in the press. In all likelihood, reporters, like just about everyone else in Washington, believed that Carswell could not be defeated, and saw little reason to cover what probably looked like nothing more than another futile speech on behalf of a lost cause. But Mary McGrory devoted her column in the Washington *Evening Star* the following day to the episode. Observing that "the most powerful speech against the Carswell nomination to the Supreme Court was the least attended," she went on to say that "few Republicans wanted to hear the Senate's only black member eloquently laying out the case against Carswell and removing, one by one, the props they are leaning on to justify a vote for a Southern judge whose partisans have admitted is mediocre."

That few senators were on the floor at the time was by no means uncommon. While many senators claim that they carefully read the preceding day's business in the *Congressional Record* each morning to make sure that they are abreast of current developments, it is unlikely that more than a handful of them actually do. Unfortunately, some of the most crucial speeches pass unnoticed unless the newspapers pick them up and alert other members of the Senate to what took place on the floor during their absence. Miss McGrory's column made up for the daily reporters' omission, and made it certain that word of the speech would now reach Brooke's colleagues and prompt them to read it in the *Record*.

A more immediate result of Brooke's speech was that Hatfield, Percy, and Mathias were clearly, if unhappily, impressed by it. As for Bayh, when he returned to his office after listening to the speech he summoned his staff and said, "If we really mean what we're saying about the Voting Rights Act and all these other civil-rights matters, how can we let Carswell go through without making a fight?" None of his aides had an answer, so he instructed them to prepare material against the nomination in case he got into the fight all the way, and also to draw up the best arguments they could make against his working openly to defeat the nomination.

When they met with him to discuss their conclusions on the latter subject, four days later, three of them—Robert Keefe, his administrative assistant and top aide; Joseph Rees, Keefe's deputy; and Bill Wise, Bayh's press officer—argued that by this time Carswell had been shown to be so poor a choice for a seat on the Supreme Court that the Senator could not conceivably be hurt politically if he fought the nomination.

But two others—P. J. Mode and Jason Berman, who worked on the Subcommittee on Constitutional Amendments, of which Bayh was chairman—disagreed with this view. For some time, they had been deeply involved in Bayh's attempt to push his

Constitutional amendment abolishing the Electoral College and setting up direct election of the President and Vice-President through the Judiciary Committee and onto the Senate floor for a vote. They argued that it was going to be exceedingly difficult to get the amendment approved by two-thirds of the members of the Senate as required, and that he had no hope of accomplishing this without the support of moderate Republicans, who would probably resent it if he tried to force them to oppose their President again on a Supreme Court nomination. In addition, Mode and Berman pointed out, there was the threat of a filibuster over the amendment on the part of Southerners who opposed it because they believed it would destroy the balance of power they would hold in the event of an electoral standoff in a Presidential election. While Senator Strom Thurmond, the Democrat-turned-Dixiecrat-turned-Republican from South Carolina, could be expected to lead such a filibuster, he couldn't sustain it by himself and would need the help of other Southerners. If Bayh were to make *them* angry enough by attacking Carswell, men like Senator James O. Eastland, Democrat of Mississippi and chairman of the Judiciary Committee, who opposed direct election but not to the point of being willing to wage an all-out fight against it, might well pull out all the stops and go after him on his amendment. Mode and Berman made it clear that they, too, opposed the Carswell nomination, but saw no chance of defeating it and no point in jeopardizing a likely cause for a lost one.

These arguments troubled Bayh, for he was deeply committed to his amendment. If it was adopted, he would achieve national prominence, and there were reports that he was contemplating a race for the Presidency. Besides, he saw little hope that enough senators would stand up against Carswell's nomination to make a good showing, let alone to defeat it. In short, Bayh might lose both battles and hurt himself in the process. Even so, when the meeting ended most members of his staff were convinced that, as Keefe later put it, "he had decided to go." But he was still unwilling to say so openly, and for the time being he left the matter there.

It was still there a week later when Bayh arrived at the Statler Hilton Hotel, in the capital, to attend an emergency meeting of the Leadership Conference on Civil Rights, a loose confederation of a hundred and twenty-seven groups that functioned largely as a lobbying operation. The meeting had been called mainly to devise tactics in the battle against the Administration's attempts to dismantle the Voting Rights Act, but before much discussion of that subject took place the question of Judge Carswell's nomination came up. One of the speakers at the session that evening was Senator Joseph D. Tydings, Democrat of Maryland, who had agreed, tentatively and reluctantly, to lead the fight against Carswell— tentatively because he hoped someone else would take over the leadership, and reluctantly because he was up for reelection in the fall and didn't need any more enemies than he had. So far, Tydings had been working out of the public eye, chiefly to marshal opposition and delay the vote on confirming or rejecting the nominee. For the past few days, the Senator had been walking around with a temperature of a hundred and one degrees, and when he rose to speak about Carswell he was neither encouraging nor persuasive about the chances of defeating him. As soon as Tydings finished, he left the hotel.

Fifteen minutes later, when Bayh arrived to speak, he was unaware of what had gone on before he got there. He spoke for a time on the Voting Rights Act, and then, in an extemporaneous digression, he launched into a free-swinging attack on Carswell's nomination. The audience was with Bayh from the start, and as he warmed up they stayed with him. In conclusion, he shouted that Carswell not only could be defeated but *had* to be defeated, and the audience rose to its feet and stamped, cheered, whistled, and applauded for several minutes.

Afterward, Keefe said, "The Senator turned them on, and their response turned him on." When Bayh arrived at his office the following morning, he was clearly very much turned on. Calling in his staff and several outsiders who had been waiting for a Senate leader to emerge against the Carswell nomination, he talked briefly about which senators could be relied on for speeches against Carswell when the floor debate on the nomination began. Once that was settled, he got up from his desk, smiled, and said, "O.K., let's crank it up."

The crank had already been forged, tempered, and put into place. One of the people who had been working on it and hoping for a chance to use it was an attractive young Negro lawyer, Mrs. Marian Wright Edelman, who had come up from the South to take a degree at the Yale Law School and then had become director of the Washington Research Project, a civil-rights outfit in the capital, and a member of its Action Council. When Carswell was nominated, Mrs. Edelman knew more about him than most other people in Washington. The summer before, when President Nixon elevated him from the District Court to the Fifth Circuit Court of Appeals, she had helped circulate a memorandum put out by the Legal Defense and Educational Fund opposing that nomination, and the memorandum had been submitted by the Leadership Conference, with the concurrence of the A.F.L.-C.I.O., to the Judiciary Committee. The committee's hearings on Carswell's promotion to the Court of Appeals lasted only ten minutes, however, and it was approved by the Senate without a dissenting vote. "To an extent, this was the fault of civil-rights groups, which hadn't been doing enough preventive work," Mrs. Edelman explained later. "Carswell's nomination to the Fifth Circuit Court of Appeals was one more tactic in the Attorney General's Southern strategy, and we're on the verge of losing our pro-civil-rights majority on that court. Anyway, if something had been done then, Carswell wouldn't have got on that court, let alone have been named to the Supreme Court."

The day Carswell's nomination to the highest court was announced, Mrs Edelman telephoned several lawyers she knew in Florida to see what else she could find out about the nominee. "The first one I got through to told me that he was a bad guy," she recalled later. "The others told me he was a *really* bad guy. Initially, I didn't believe we could defeat him. I just thought we had to get twenty or thirty or however many votes we could muster, because it was vital to show black people where this man stood and to demonstrate that a large part of the Senate opposed him. What galled me so much is this Administration's disregard for our institutions. For people who talk about law and order all the time, this disrespect for our institutions, including even the Supreme Court, is staggering. To use all of them for political ends, as Nixon has done time after time, is horribly destructive to our system. Anyway, I knew we needed—all of us needed—a psychological lift. If we could even slow him down, that would do it."

As the first step toward slowing down the President, Mrs. Edelman sent an assistant, Richard Seymour, to Tallahassee to see what he could find out for the Action Council. Before he got there, Ed Roeder, a reporter for WJXT-TV, in Jacksonville, Florida, uncovered Carswell's 1948 speech in the files of the now defunct Irwinton, Georgia, *Bulletin*. A couple of days later, Seymour came up with an equally impressive document—the papers changing the public golf course into a private club, with Carswell's signature on them as an incorporator. As soon as Mrs. Edelman read the incorporation papers and saw their implication, she showed them to Joseph L. Rauh, Jr., a lawyer in private practice in Washington who was counsel to the Leadership Conference, vice-chairman of the Americans for Democratic Action, and a veteran of innumerable human- and civil-rights wars over the past quarter of a century. Two days before the Senate hearings on the nomination began, Rauh knew, the American Bar Association's twelve-man Committee on the Federal Judiciary was scheduled to meet to consider—or, rather, to go through the motions of considering—whether it should endorse him.

No one anticipated anything but a unanimous recommendation, because the committee had endorsed every Supreme Court nominee, including Haynsworth, since it was set up, fourteen years before. In general, the committee was firmly in the grasp of its chairman, Lawrence E. Walsh, who not only was close to the President, having been his personal representative at the Paris peace talks for some months, but had been Deputy Attorney General, the official responsible for recommending judges for the federal bench, in 1958, when Carswell was named to the District Court. Still, Rauh felt there might be a chance that other members of the committee would break loose from Walsh's hold if the evidence against Carswell was compelling. With this in mind, Rauh took the papers to one of the committee members he knew, Charles A. Horsky, also a Washington attorney, and Horsky promised to look them over and show them to the committee when it met.

Perhaps more than anyone else in Washington, Rauh was bewildered at first by the President's choice. Shortly before Carswell's name was announced by the White House, Rauh was told by a couple of reporters who the nominee was going to be. He refused to believe them and argued that the Administration would not dare choose a man who had been opposed for a lesser post by such a powerful coalition as the civil-rights and labor movements. He pointed out that the White House could scarcely have been unaware of this opposition, since it was a part of the official record, which would have been read by anyone who was investigating Carswell's background, and since, furthermore, the memorandum submitted to the Senate Judiciary Committee had been prominently reported by the Washington *Post* at the time. The reporters went off to look up that account, which appeared on June 12, 1969, and which stated, in part:

> In a memorandum to the Senate Judiciary Committee, the Leadership Conference said Carswell has shown "a strong bias against Negroes asserting civil rights claims" in his 11 years on the bench. Carswell, 49, "has been more hostile to civil rights cases than any other federal judge in Florida," the memorandum said, adding a plea for more liberal judges in view of the Fifth Circuit's heavy load of civil rights cases. . . .
>
> The Court has expanded from nine members to an authorized strength of 15, but it continues to be deeply and closely divided on some sensitive race issues. The Circuit divided 6-to-6 in a faculty desegregation case from Montgomery, Ala., only to be told last week by an unanimous Supreme Court to press harder for total elimination of dual-race school systems. . . . The memorandum said the judge was unceremoniously reversed by the Fifth Circuit as "clearly in error" for approving an inadequate school desegregation plan and refusing to consider issues of faculty and staff desegregation. It charged that his delays in a school lawsuit for Leon County (Fla.) held up progress there for three years.

Then the reporters read the memorandum itself, discussed its contents with members of the Administration, and came back to Rauh and told him that the White House had indeed been aware of the position taken by the Leadership Conference and the unions but would not be swayed by it. "The White House didn't know then about the 1948 speech or the golf club," Rauh said recently. "But they knew about our opposition, and I believe they actually *hoped* for it. The President didn't want to lose again, of course, but he wanted to win with opposition from the same people who had fought him on Haynsworth. He wanted to defeat his enemies in face-to-face combat. Lots of Southerners would have been confirmed easily, and he knew it. But he chose the only man whom the Leadership Conference had ever opposed for the federal bench—except Haynsworth when he was named to the Supreme Court. Also, it wasn't just that we *might* oppose Carswell again but that we *had* to, because of our earlier stand. And that was equally true of labor. That's taking on a lot of enemies. They were willing to take all of us on because they were convinced they couldn't be beaten again."

A few hours before Carswell's nomination was announced, Attorney General Mitchell briefed Republican leaders of the Senate and Republican members of the Judiciary Committee on the Judge's background and record. Although Mitchell must have known about the strong opposition that the nomination would inevitably create, he said nothing about it on this occasion. Instead, he concentrated on three points: that Carswell had nothing in his record suggesting any economic conflicts of interests like those which had brought Haynsworth down, that he had no stigma of anti-labor bias that might turn the unions against him, and that he was a "moderate" on civil rights. Then, simultaneously with the White House announcement of the nomination, Senator Roman Hruska, an arch-conservative Republican from Nebraska who had an almost unblemished record of defending unsavory causes and who had been chosen by the Administration to defend this one, briefed all the Republican members of the Senate who were in town and free. He made the same points that Mitchell had, and when the session broke up, several senators emerged to tell reporters who were waiting outside that they were satisfied about Judge Carswell's fitness for the Supreme Court and would vote to confirm him.

The most important of these was Senator Hugh Scott, of Pennsylvania, the Minority Leader. Since he had already attended the briefing by Mitchell, presumably he went to the second one so he could exert his influence on other Republicans by his emphatic assurance, in the presence of the press, that he supported the nominee "without qualification." Scott's statement was thought at the time to be possibly crucial—perhaps as crucial, in fact, as his earlier opposition to Haynsworth, which had made it easier for other Republicans to vote the same way.

As it happened, no one in the Administration had told Scott about the stand that was certain to be taken by civil-rights and labor groups—a significant omission, since he was up for reëlection and, given the nature of his highly industrialized constituency, he knew he would have trouble winning against the active opposition of both groups. At the time, Scott had no reason to suspect that the Administration had misled him, and he had good reason to support its choice for the Court. His vote against Haynsworth had naturally endangered his position as Minority Leader because it constituted a major break with the Administration. That might have been acceptable once, but it would not be twice—not twice in a row, anyway. Also, of course, he hoped that his endorsement of Carswell would mollify conservatives back home who were after his scalp because of the part he played in the Haynsworth affair. And, finally, it seemed certain to him that the F.B.I., still smarting from the recriminations that followed its haphazard investigation in that case, would have peered into every cranny of Carswell's life before the President chose him. In short, Scott wanted to accept Carswell because he had to.

Other Republicans, though, didn't have to, and some of them were inclined to view the situation rather differently.

Brooke, for one, was amazed at Scott's hasty endorsement. As he saw it, the F.B.I.'s failure to uncover Haynsworth's improprieties on the bench suggested not so much assurance that it would do the job properly the next time as proof that there was something wrong with the investigative mechanism itself. Moreover, there was the record of the Attorney General to consider, and Brooke found little in it to comfort black citizens or anyone who was concerned about the welfare of black citizens.

Another Republican, Senator Mathias, was also reluctant to accept Mitchell's appraisal of Carswell. After the briefing, Mathias returned to his office and dug out a confidential memorandum that his staff had prepared during the contention over Haynsworth and that had been distributed among a dozen or so moderate and liberal Republicans at the time. The memorandum, which was dated November 5, 1969, said, in part:

> As moderate Republicans appointed by Eisenhower retire from the Fifth Circuit and as Haynsworth prepares to leave the Fourth, the Nixon Administration is choosing segregationist Democrats or Dixicans to replace them. Since these judges are being named by Mitchell and approved in a perfunctory way, Nixon may well not be fully aware of their record or probable impact.
>
> The most recent appointee, pushed through the Senate Judiciary Committee and confirmed on the floor on Moratorium Day, is Charles Clark, a leading strategist in Mississippi's resistance to desegregation and close associate of William Harold Cox, segregationist District Court Judge. . . .
>
> Nixon's other recent appointee to this crucial court, George Harrold Carswell, of Florida, is described by Southern lawyers as an even more unfortunate choice than Clark, since Carswell is older, less intelligent, and more set in his ways. As a district judge, he has been repeatedly reversed and reproached by the Fifth Circuit for his rulings in cases involving desegregation of everything from reform schools to theaters. But his chief tech-

nique, say civil-rights lawyers, is prolonged temporization. . . .

These appointments come at a time when the Administration has adopted a policy of channeling most civil-rights enforcement through the Courts. [They come] at a time when Southern blacks, though still more optimistic about the pace of change than Northerners, are growing increasingly militant and dissatisfied. If Nixon continues with such appointments, we can expect increasing black despair about the judicial process in the South and increasing resort to violence. The Haynsworth appointment seems to be part of a general pattern of judicial nominations that threatens to change the character of the Southern Courts of Appeal system, which in the past has been favorable to civil rights.

"The memo also got to the White House at the time," Mathias said not long ago. "So they knew over there that they were bound to create division over here when they sent up Carswell's name."

The contents of the Leadership Conference and Mathias memoranda suggested that the Administration was indeed confident that the Senate would accept *any* nominee. These documents also suggested that the White House had intentionally misled Scott—perhaps in the hope that by creating an unresolvable political dilemma for him it could diminish his prestige and then move in to replace him as its spokesman in the Senate. Of course, before the Southern strategy could prevail there Scott would have to go, for in his twenty-six years in Congress he had supported, and had been supported by, the black voters in his constituency, and could not be expected to turn against them now.

In the days immediately following the nomination, Mrs. Edelman talked with several more lawyers, some who practiced in Florida and others who worked for the Department of Justice and had appeared before Judge Carswell on behalf of the government. "They made it clear that he was a terrible guy—worse than we'd been told before," she has recalled.

"These reports made us even more desperate. We were panicked by the press of time. For instance, one of our problems
was finding witnesses and conducting a thorough investigation during the eight-day period between the announcement
of the nomination and the opening of the hearings. It was
perfectly clear by then—after the 1948 speech and the golf-
club episode—that the F.B.I. had done an even sloppier job
on Carswell than it had on Haynsworth. It was also perfectly
clear that many senators would be extremely embarrassed if
they came out for Carswell and then more damaging facts
about his past were revealed. But Eastland was determined
to ram the nomination through, and he refused to grant a postponement. Also, we knew that we had to stir up an immense
amount of outside opposition to bring enough senators over
to our side, and that this would take time. Then, there were
the questions: Was the Leadership Conference going to fight
or just make a statement and let it go at that? What were
the unions going to do? Who was going to lead the opposition
in the Senate? Which would take priority there—revision of
the Voting Rights Act, which was coming up for a vote, or
Carswell? Could we use the same people to fight both at the
same time? How could we get the key senators smoked out?
How could we get a bipartisan start? How could we persuade
the press to do investigative work for us? How could we get
stuff out to the public at large? How could we circulate the
basic material on the Hill and make sure it was read?"

Or, as Senator Bayh later put it, "The problem was simple
and at the same time monumental—how do you create enough
counterpressure to neutralize the natural pressure created by
the President's backing so that senators are free to decide the
issue on the merits?"

On the day that Carswell's nomination was announced by
the White House, Rauh put out a brief statement for the

A.D.A. saying that the Judge's "principal qualification for the post seems to be his opposition to Negro rights," and that "while this may be good Nixon-Mitchell politics in the suburbs and the South, it can only add to the already dangerous racial tensions in America." Rauh was instantly denounced by some for responding in the usual knee-jerk liberal fashion—a response that Carswell's defenders put down to blind prejudice against all Southerners. Of course, since Rauh had opposed Carswell's elevation to the Court of Appeals, he could not fail now to oppose his elevation to the Supreme Court. To an extent, though, the charge was valid when it came to many of Carswell's earliest opponents, for they had set out to find something improper in his record almost as soon as his name and his residence were announced As time wore on, though, and the case against Carswell grew, his friends seemed to find nothing more to offer in his defense than the prejudice of his enemies.

In any event, two days after Rauh's statement the N.A.A.C.P. also came out against the nomination, on the ground that it was "clearly designed to compromise the Negroes' future judicial protection far beyond the life of any single Administration," and the New York *Times* ran an editorial calling the nomination "a shock" and adding that it "almost suggests an intention to reduce the significance of the Court by lowering the caliber of its membership." The same day, the *Times* published an interview with Professor Leroy D. Clark, of New York University, who had formerly been the head of the Legal Defense and Educational Fund in northern Florida. Professor Clark charged that Carswell had invariably handed down improper decisions after creating improper delays, and concluded, "It was my view that of the federal district judges I appeared before Harrold Carswell was clearly the most openly and blatantly segregationist."

On January 23rd, staff members of four liberal Democrats on the Judiciary Committee—Senators Bayh, Kennedy, Tydings, and Hart—met in Bayh's office with a number of others who were upset about the nomination. For the most part, it was the same group that had fought the Haynsworth nomination. Among the aides were Bayh's men Keefe and Rees; James Flug, a young lawyer who worked for Kennedy; Lee Miller, also a young lawyer, from Tydings' office; and Bert Wides, an assistant to Hart. Among the outsiders were Mrs. Edelman; Rauh; Verlin Nelson, lobbyist for the A.D.A.; Clarence Mitchell, head of the Washington branch of the N.A.A.C.P. and, with Rauh, the moving force behind the Leadership Conference; Andrew Biemiller and Thomas Harris, lobbyists for the A.F.L.-C.I.O.; and Brad Brasfield, of the United Auto Workers.

The meeting was brief and revolved largely around the question of which senator, preferably a prominent one, might be persuaded to lead a full-fledged attack on the nomination. At the moment, Bayh seemed to be out, because no one present, including his aides, expected him to wage another exhausting—and, this time, unpromising—battle so soon after

36

the Haynsworth affair. Kennedy was still under the cloud of doubts raised by the accident at Chappaquiddick. Tydings was not eager to add new enemies to his old ones just before election time, and preferred to restrict the leadership role he had partially accepted to working out of the public's view rather than taking on the nominee openly. And Hart, who was also up for reëlection, had led the struggle to get Abe Fortas confirmed as Chief Justice before *his* improprieties on the bench were revealed, and was in no position now to attack another nominee. In the end, the participants did little more than reach a general agreement that if a leader could be found they would work with him as they had worked with Bayh against Haynsworth.

Flug seemed to be the one person at the meeting who felt that Carswell could be not only strongly opposed by the Senate but actually defeated, and the next day he sent Kennedy a memorandum outlining the emerging case against Carswell. "Nixon-Mitchell have again nominated a mediocre candidate with no indications of particular intelligence, leadership, insight, or respect among his brethren," Flug wrote. "In fact, his official record is quite consistent with the notion that he is a segregationist and white-supremacist." He reported that evidence to buttress this last point was being compiled and would be ready for the Senator's perusal soon, and then he added, "The civil-rights groups and the unorganized black community are, of course, really upset. Roy Wilkins is outraged. . . . The unions say they are not particularly interested, that they can't find anything anti-union in his record . . . that they're too busy to do much."

Flug went on to inform Kennedy that LeRoy Collins, the former Democratic governor of Florida, who was expected to be the most prominent witness for Carswell at the hearings on his nomination, "has been calling around saying what a great guy and civil-rights moderate Carswell is, but when challenged has admitted that Carswell really isn't Supreme Court calibre and that he (Collins) hasn't actually looked at Carswell's civil-rights opinions." After suggesting that Kennedy might join Bayh and Hart in a personal appeal they intended to make to Eastland to postpone the hearings, so that Senate investigators could do the job that the F.B.I. had fumbled, and that Kennedy might also persuade Scott to reconsider his hasty endorsement, Flug wound up by proposing a series of questions that the Senator might ask Carswell when the hearings convened.

A few hours after Flug gave his boss the memorandum, a telephone call came into Tydings' office from a man who refused to identify himself but said he had some information that could be useful to Tydings if he intended to oppose Carswell. Ultimately, the call was put through to Stanley Mazaroff, another young lawyer on Tydings' staff, and the man explained that his name was Norman Knopf, that he was one of the Senator's constituents, and that in 1964, shortly after graduating from law school, he had served as a summer volunteer under a Justice Department program helping civil-rights lawyers who were working on voter-registration cases in Florida. During that summer, he went on, he had personally seen Carswell temporize, insult lawyers and witnesses for the government, and generally obstruct civil-rights cases. Mazaroff assured Knopf that Tydings would be interested in what he had to say, and asked whether he would be willing to discuss his experience in person with the Senator. Knopf, his voice shaking, said that he couldn't do that, but Mazaroff kept talking and finally persuaded him at least to give his home telephone number.

On January 25th, the day after this call, the *Times* printed a letter from John Lowenthal, a professor of law at Rutgers University, one of the volunteer civil-rights lawyers who had gone to Florida to assist in the voter-registration drive during the 1964 Presidential campaign, and who now wrote that Judge Carswell had made persistent attempts to impede the progress of Negro registration. As it happened, Lowenthal was one of the lawyers whom Knopf mentioned he had worked for, and when Tydings was told about the telephone call and the letter he instructed Mazaroff to ask Knopf to come by for a talk. Mazaroff called Knopf at home that night, and when he explained that Tydings wanted to talk over Knopf's experiences in Judge Carswell's court Knopf expressed extreme reluctance to get involved. Finally, he explained why—he worked for the Department of Justice. After some more conversation, however, he hesitantly agreed to come over to Tydings' office a few days later. But he refused to testify at the hearings unless he was forced to under a subpoena.

On the same day, the American Bar Association's Committee on the Federal Judiciary met in New York to consider Carswell's nomination, and the next evening, while ten of the committee's twelve members were discussing it, the two others, Horsky and Norman P. Ramsey, paid a visit to Carswell, who was staying at the Sheraton-Park Hotel in Washington, to discuss his part in incorporating the golf club. Horsky showed him the papers that Rauh had passed on and went over them with the Judge in detail to find out what, exactly, his role had been. In the end, they accepted his explanation that he had been an incorporator of the private club but had not participated in its management, and, in fact, had not retained his membership very long. Satisfied with this, Horsky assured Carswell that the committee would endorse him, and that same night it did, by a unanimous vote.

Through a coincidence of timing, Rauh, who was certain that timing would determine the outcome of the issue, had that very afternoon given a reporter from the Washington *Post* the details about Carswell's part in setting up a segregated club while he was serving as U.S. Attorney, and the paper ran the story on the front page in the next morning's early edition. For the time being, though, nothing was reported about Horsky's and Ramsey's visit to Carswell the night before.

Senator Eastland having turned down all pleas for a postponement of the hearings on the nomination, they opened in the Senate Judiciary Committee chamber as scheduled, at a little after ten-thirty on the morning of January 27th, the day the *Post* story appeared. The nominee was to be the first witness, and he sat waiting as the two senators from Florida and the representative from Tallahassee delivered the usual encomiums. All but one of the seventeen members of the Judiciary Committee were present—the absentee being Senator Mathias, who was in Europe on Senate business—and, undoubtedly, all those present had read the story in the *Post*.

Senator Hruska was the first member of the committee to question Carswell, and he brought up the matter of the golf club at once, apparently in the hope that he might establish a strong defense for Carswell before opposing senators got to question him. "Now, this morning's paper had some mention that you were a member of a country club down in Tallahassee," Hruska said. "I am confident that you read the account. I would be safe in saying all of us did. You are entitled to tell your side of the story and tell us just what the facts are."

Carswell replied that he had "read the story very hurriedly." Several members of the committee looked surprised at this casual handling of so serious a matter, but, of course, none of them knew that there had been little need for the Judge to study the newspaper account, since he had spent part of the evening before going over the original documents. While Bayh, Kennedy, Tydings, and Hart were aware that Horsky had the incorporating papers, at this stage they did not know that he had met with Carswell, let alone that he had shown Carswell the papers and that Carswell had conceded his involvement as an incorporator. In any event, it was clear that they would not let the witness pass off the question so indifferently. But before any of them could break into the discussion, Carswell finally said, "The import of this thing, as I understand it, was that I had something to do with taking the public lands to keep a segregated facility. I have never had any discussion with any human being about the subject of this at all. That is the totality of it, Senators. I know no more about it than that."

"Were you an incorporator of that club, as was alleged in one of the accounts I read?" Hruska asked.

"No, sir," Carswell answered.

A little later, Hruska asked, "Could the stock [in the club] you received on this occasion have borne the label 'incorporator,' indicating that you were one of the contributors to the building fund for the clubhouse?"

"Perhaps," Judge Carswell replied. "I have no personal recollection."

At another point, Hruska asked, "Are you, or were you at the time, familiar with the bylaws or the articles of incorporation?"

"No, sir," Carswell answered.

About an hour later, Senator Kennedy began questioning

the Judge about the golf-club episode, and as he proceeded it became clear from the words he used that he had a copy of the incorporating papers before him. This produced a different effect. When Kennedy asked the witness if he had signed the letter of incorporation for the club, the answer was direct and explicit. "Yes, sir. I recall that," Carswell said. Kennedy went on to inquire whether he had read the paper first, and Carswell replied, "Certainly I read it, Senator. I am sure I must have. I would read anything before I put my signature on it, I think." The belated admission that he had read and signed the incorporating papers was later cited repeatedly by his supporters as evidence that he had not deceived, or been less than candid with, the committee, which ultimately became the gravest charge against him.

However, those who took this position ignored a colloquy during the following day's hearing, two days after Horsky had shown the Judge the papers in question, when Bayh said, "Since you have looked at the documents, I suppose—" and Carswell quickly broke in to say, "Senator, I have not looked at the documents. I didn't mean to leave that impression with you. The documents speak for themselves. I couldn't begin to tell you what the documents say." A couple of minutes later, he added, "I think the records will show—I have not examined them, but I am positive that I have never been any incorporator, director, whatever the language may be on there. I have never participated in any corporation that ever took any action with regard to anything."

Carswell also repeatedly insisted that he had been unaware that the private club was organized to keep Negroes out, and although many people were willing at that time to accept his denial that he had helped set up the club, it would have been difficult to find anyone who believed that he hadn't known why it was set up. His deception on this score dismayed even the staunchest conservatives, including the right-wing columnist for the Washington *Evening Star* James Kilpatrick, who described Carswell's testimony on this point as an "evasive account," and added, "He took an active role, not a passive role, in transfer of the Tallahassee municipal golf course to a private club. Forgive my incredulity, but if Carswell didn't understand the racial purpose of this legal legerdemain, he was the only one in north Florida who didn't understand it."

After three days of hearings, President Nixon held a press conference, and in the course of it he was asked whether he had been aware of the golf-club episode when he chose Carswell. Mr. Nixon replied that he hadn't, and went on, "If everybody in government service who has belonged to, or does belong to, restricted golf clubs were to leave the service, this city would have the highest rate of unemployment of any city in the country." Of course, membership in the club was not the point of the accusation, which rested on whether Carswell, then the federal government's highest law-enforcement official in the area, had violated his oath to uphold the Constitution by helping to circumvent the Supreme Court's interpretation of it.

At the start of the hearings, Senator Eastland put the American Bar Association committee's endorsement in the record, along with letters of support from roughly a third of Carswell's colleagues on the Court of Appeals. The most significant of these was from Judge Elbert B. Tuttle, who had been chief judge of the Fifth Circuit from 1961 until his retirement, in 1967, and who was regarded as one of the most eminent jurists on the entire federal bench. In his letter, which was dated January 22nd, Judge Tuttle explained, "My purpose in writing is that I wish to make myself available to appear before the

committee at its hearing on the nomination of Judge Carswell, in support of his confirmation." At seven o'clock in the
morning before the second day's session convened, Carswell
received a telephone call from Judge Tuttle, who told him
that because of the facts that had been divulged since the
nomination was announced he felt compelled to withdraw his
offer to testify on Carswell's behalf.

When Tuttle's withdrawal became known, some weeks later,
Carswell was blamed for not having revealed it at the hearings
on the day it was made, or subsequently, to stop his supporters from citing the endorsement, as they did repeatedly to
demonstrate that their man was deeply respected by such a
leading jurist. Actually, the fault lay not only with Carswell
but with Tuttle. Like Horsky, who knew from newspaper reports of the hearings that the nominee had lied to the Judiciary
Committee the morning after meeting with him and yet said
nothing at the time, Judge Tuttle kept his silence.

During the third day of the hearing, Knopf, the reluctant
Justice Department attorney, finally appeared in Tydings'
office to talk things over. Mazaroff took him to an empty room
next to the Judiciary Committee chamber and then went to
the hearing room to inform Tydings, who immediately joined
Knopf. Within a few minutes, he corroborated, in far greater
detail, what Professor Lowenthal had described in his letter
to the *Times*. "The moment I talked to Knopf, I just erupted,"
Tydings said afterward. "Knopf made it clear that Carswell
not only was a segregationist but wasn't even good at his job.
The idea of seeing a man like Carswell go on the Supreme
Court was too much for me. Even after our conversation,
though, I didn't think there was a chance of defeating him.
I just hoped to get as much on the record as I could, to use
in the floor debate and in defense of my vote when I was

attacked for it, as I was sure to be, in my campaign for re-election."

Professor Lowenthal appeared at the hearings to testify about how Carswell had both resisted civil-rights progress and mistreated those who tried to achieve it. He confined himself to one experience—a case involving seven civil-rights volunteers who were arrested on charges of criminal trespass in August, 1964, as they went about northern Florida trying to get Negroes to register to vote in the coming election. Civil-rights attorneys on the scene—mainly Northerners who came South for a month or two each—believed that they could not hope for a fair trial in a local court, so they obtained a federal court order removing the case from the Gadsden County court to Judge Carswell's court in Tallahassee. However, the local judge simply ignored the removal order, ejected the lawyers from his courtroom, refused the defendants time to get other counsel, and then tried, convicted, and jailed them.

"At that point, or early the next morning at 2 A.M., I arrived in Tallahassee, and it was obvious that since my clients were now in jail, the first move was habeas corpus, so I prepared habeas-corpus petitions at once," Lowenthal testified. "It was evident to all those with experience in northern Florida that it was not safe for voter-registration people to be in local jails. Moreover, the voter-registration drive was stalled while the workers were in jail, and the local blacks were intimidated from registering." Continuing, he described how Judge Carswell refused to accept the habeas-corpus papers and demanded that they be redone on special forms, available only in his court. That in itself was of doubtful legal validity, and so was the Judge's requirement that the forms be signed by the defendants. Since Lowenthal was more concerned about the safety of his clients than he was about quibbling over details, he drove the twenty-five miles to the local jail, only to find that the volunteers had been sent out on a road-work gang, another twenty-five miles distant. Finally, he telephoned Judge Carswell and got him to agree to accept the papers without the defendants' signatures.

The next step was a habeas-corpus hearing in the Judge's chambers—a curious affair, as it turned out, because the representative of the state, the local prosecutor, refused to appear. As for the Judge, Lowenthal went on, "I can only describe his attitude as being extremely hostile. . . . Judge Carswell indicated that he would try his best to deny the habeas-corpus petitions, but I pointed out that he had no discretion in the matter, that the Gadsden County officials had clearly acted in derogation of Judge Carswell's own jurisdiction, since the removal to Judge Carswell's court was wholly proper." Although the point was elementary, Judge Carswell refused to accede to it, and sent his clerk off for some lawbooks. Finally, after studying the federal statute in question, he granted the petition, but he refused to have the order served by the U.S. marshal, as required under law, and told Lowenthal to deliver it himself.

None too anxious to put himself in the hands of the local sheriff, Lowenthal nevertheless saw that he had little choice, and took it to the sheriff, who accepted it with surprising amiability and released the prisoners. They were on their way down the courthouse steps with Lowenthal when the sheriff reappeared, all amiability gone, and rearrested them. As it turned out, Judge Carswell, on his own motion and without any notice to the defendants or a hearing to give them an opportunity to present testimony and arguments on their behalf, had remanded the case to the Gadsden County court and had notified the sheriff before the defendants left. "All the little ways in which a federal district judge can make life difficult seemed to me to be in force," Lowenthal told the committee.

Deciding that it would be helpful to corroborate Lowenthal's testimony, Tydings put in an official request to have a committee subpoena served on Knopf, who still refused to appear voluntarily as a witness. Before granting the request, Eastland called Tydings and said, "Joe, you don't want to use that boy. He's bad news." Taken aback, Tydings got the impression that Eastland had something from F.B.I. files on Knopf, and told Mazaroff about the remark. Mazaroff visited Knopf at his home and went over everything in his past and his personal life that could possibly be used in the hearings to embarrass him—and Tydings. All that Knopf could come up with was that he had once attended an S.D.S. meeting out of curiosity, so Tydings went ahead and called him as a witness.

Once Knopf was on the stand, he was eager to volunteer all the information he could. "This was my first courtroom experience, really, out of law school, and I remember quite clearly Judge Carswell," he told the committee. "He didn't talk to me directly. He addressed himself to the lawyer, of course, Mr. Lowenthal, who explained what the habeas-corpus writ was about, and I can only say that there was extreme hostility between the Judge and Mr. Lowenthal. Judge Carswell made clear, when he found out that he was a Northern volunteer and that there were some [other] Northern volunteers down, that he did not approve of any of this voter registration going on, and he was especially critical of Mr. Lowenthal—in fact, he lectured him for a long time in a high voice that made me start thinking I was glad I filed a bond for protection in case I got thrown in jail. I really thought we were all going to be held in contempt of court. It was a very long, strict lecture about Northern lawyers coming down . . . and meddling down here and arousing the local people against —rather, just arousing the local people—and he in effect didn't want any part of this, and he made it quite clear that he was going to deny all relief that we requested."

The Judiciary Committee's hearings on Carswell's nomination were spread out over two weeks, and during the weekend that intervened Tydings became increasingly distressed at the thought of Carswell's sitting on the Supreme Court. The prospect was so unsettling that on Saturday night the Senator had trouble sleeping and got up very early on Sunday. At eight o'clock that morning, he summoned several members of his staff to his office and told them that more had to be done to create opposition to Carswell's nomination. One of them recalled that Knopf had told him about a man named Ernst Rosenberger, a lawyer in private practice in New York, who had also worked on civil-rights cases in Florida just before the 1964 election. The aide called him, and Rosenberger agreed to tell of his experiences in Judge Carswell's court. Another aide got in touch with Leroy Clark, the former head of the Legal Defense and Educational Fund in Florida, whose views on Carswell's racial bias had been reported earlier by the *Times*, and he agreed to testify, too. Both men flew down to Washington and joined Tydings and his staff to discuss their testimony.

Neither man had much time to prepare himself, for they

were called to appear before the committee the following day. Rosenberger, who testified first, started out by describing the general animosity that he and other civil-rights workers had encountered in Florida—the mailman refused to deliver mail to the house where they lived and worked because the mailbox was set six inches behind the line of other mailboxes on the street; a deputy sheriff regularly tore down posters carrying appeals for Negroes to register to vote; volunteers were refused service in restaurants; they were assaulted, and firebombs were set off under their automobiles; and, when all this failed to intimidate them, shots were fired through the windows of their house.

Continuing, Rosenberger described how nine clergymen who had been arrested for unlawful assembly for trying to integrate a Florida airport had been denied release on habeas-corpus writs by Judge Carswell. Rosenberger appealed the Judge's decision to the Court of Appeals, and three of its judges came to Tallahassee to hear arguments on the case. Those took up one morning, and that afternoon Rosenberger, who was in Carswell's chambers, heard him suggest to the prosecuting attorney that he could settle the case at once by getting the local judge to reduce the clergymen's sentences to the time already served. This would mean that they would immediately be let out of jail and then would have no legal standing to file a writ of habeas corpus, the purpose of which, of course, is to get one out of jail.

The following day, the prosecutor called Rosenberger to his office and suggested that he ask the local judge for a reduction of sentence. Having heard Carswell outline this plan and suspecting that it would soon be acted on, Rosenberger had already spoken to his clients about it, and they had instructed him to turn it down. When he did, the prosecutor proposed that they drop in at the local court and talk to the judge. As they entered the courtroom, Rosenberger saw that his clients were present and the court was in session. Bewildered by this turn, he sat down, and then the judge read a prepared order reducing the sentence and cited Rosenberger's request for that move.

Jumping up, Rosenberger objected. "I told him that I had made no such application, I would make no such application, and my clients did not want that application," he told the committee. "Rather, they wanted a hearing wherein they could be vindicated."

Ignoring him, the judge told the clergymen to rise, and said, "Now you have got what you came for: you have got a permanent criminal record."

When Professor Clark, speaking on behalf of the National Conference of Black Lawyers, took the stand, he assured the committee that what it had been told about Judge Carswell's persistent hostility toward civil-rights lawyers was by no means exaggerated. "Whenever I took a young lawyer into the state and he or she was to appear before Carswell, I usually spent the evening before making them go through their argument while I harassed them, as preparation for what they would meet the following day," he said. In his view, though, Carswell's animosity under these circumstances was less important than the question "Is Carswell a man who really, personally, does not like black people?" Submitting that the Judge's record on the bench proved that he did not, Clark cited case after case to buttress his contention.

One was a Florida school-desegreation case in which the Court of Appeals had unanimously rejected Carswell on both his ruling and his procedure; that, Clark said, demonstrated that Judge Carswell was either biassed or incompetent. Another was a theatre-desegregation suit in which Carswell had again been unanimously overruled by the Court of Appeals and described as being "clearly in error"—an uncommonly harsh statement for such a court to make. Still another involved four Negro children who had taken part in a sit-in demonstration and were sent to a reformatory before even being tried. To get them out, Clark sued to have the reformatory desegregated, and, as he had anticipated, the authorities released the children in order to keep the place segregated. Clark appealed, on the ground that the original suit stood as he had filed it, whereupon, as he had also anticipated, Carswell rejected his claim and said that since the defendants had been released, they had no legal standing; the Court of Appeals reversed him once again, and ordered the reformatory desegregated.

In most civil-rights cases, Clark continued, Judge Carswell principally relied on "dilatory tactics." One example concerned the school system of Leon County, Florida, where out of sixteen thousand Negro children four were permitted to attend otherwise white schools. In 1964, Clark filed a motion for further relief to remedy this situation. "We could not get a hearing, and I finally had to file a motion for a hearing," he recounted. "These hearings in other courts and before other judges when they were filed were granted as a matter of course. . . . When we got our hearing, then there was another delay before we got a ruling, and then when the ruling came it did not address itself to the basic issue in the motion—namely, a revision of the plan. Judge Carswell at that point told us that the defendants were complying with his previous order, which was not the point of the motion at all. We were saying, 'Look, this plan is not working, and it must be revised.' So we don't get a ruling. . . . We then had to file a motion asking him, 'Would you please rule on our motion?' And, finally, we got from Judge Carswell this statement . . . that no evidence could persuade the court to reorganize a desegregation plan, and evidence to that end 'would just be an idle gesture regardless of the nature of the testimony.'" After three years and the intervention of the Court of Appeals, Carswell finally granted the relief asked for.

Of the twenty witnesses who testified at the hearings, half a dozen supported the nomination. As expected, Governor Collins was the most prominent of these, and he did his best, despite his privately expressed reservations about Carswell, to defend him—for example, by pointing out that he, too, had been involved with the golf club and yet he had a long record of working for civil-rights causes. Some senators found that point persuasive, but others, like Brooke, felt that Collins' private remarks about Carswell far outweighed it. In fact, Brooke, who later read the hearing record carefully, began to wonder if anything said in Carswell's defense at the hearings had been said with conviction.

Another of Carswell's prominent supporters was James William Moore, a professor at the Yale Law School, who testified that Carswell had helped him set up the Florida State University Law School five years before and had insisted on its being "free of all racial discrimination." But then Louis H. Pollak, dean of the Yale Law School, told the committee that he had read a fair number of Carswell's opinions and had concluded that he presented "more slender credentials than any nominee for the Supreme Court put forth in this century."

55

This view was shared by another leading witness—William Van Alstyne, of the Duke University Law School, one of the most respected legal scholars in the South. Since he was a Southerner and had testified in favor of Haynsworth's nomination, Van Alstyne was not open to the charge that he would oppose anyone from the South. "There is, in candor, nothing in the quality of the nominee's work," he told the committee, "to warrant any expectation whatever that he could serve with distinction on the Supreme Court of the United States."

On the last day of the hearings, Rauh and Clarence Mitchell testified as spokesmen for the Leadership Conference on Civil Rights. Mitchell put in the record several affidavits from citizens, both white and black, of Tallahassee stating that the reason for making the municipal golf course a private club had been well known and widely discussed at the time; in fact, the subterfuge had even been written about in the local paper after a city commissioner objected to its racial implications. (The F.B.I. had also failed to look into this subject, apparently, and the affidavits had been collected by Morris Abram, Jr., a student at Harvard, who, on his own initiative and at his own expense, had gone down to Tallahassee to see what he could find out about Carswell.)

To lay the groundwork for the case that would later be made against Carswell on the floor of the Senate—that he was a mediocre judge and a racist—Rauh concentrated on fifteen cases involving civil and human rights in which Carswell had been unanimously reversed. (Subsequently, two other such cases were uncovered.) One of the few civil-rights cases that Carswell's supporters had been able to find—and cited repeatedly as evidence that he was a moderate in racial matters —was a ruling he had handed down ordering his own barber, who had a shop in a Tallahassee hotel, to take Negro customers. In reply, Rauh pointed out that Judge Carswell had actually had no alternative in that case, since the barber had conceded in his brief that his shop came under the Civil Rights Act of 1964, and had admitted, in effect, that he had violated it. "If Judge Carswell is confirmed, God help us, it will be the first time in history that a man was [sent to the Supreme Court] for writing an opinion that his rascist barber ought to cut a Negro's hair," Rauh told the committee.

In conclusion, he pleaded with the committee to extend the hearing period, and said, "If in two weeks this black record can be built by volunteers, by people with no staff, if so black a record can be built in two weeks, what could be built with an adequate investigation?" His plea was ignored, and a couple of minutes later the committee adjourned, on the order of its chairman, and went into executive session to debate and vote on the nomination.

Proof of Senator Bayh's thesis that it takes an immense effort to turn back even an obviously bad action on the part of the President emerged as soon as the hearings ended, for although the evidence submitted during them made it clear to all but the most obdurate of Carswell's supporters that he was unfit for a seat on the nation's highest court, almost no one with experience in political affairs believed that he could be stopped from getting that seat. For instance, after the hearings a story went the rounds in the Senate to the effect that Hiram L. Fong, Republican of Hawaii and a member of the Judiciary Committee, had gone up to Senator Edward J. Gurney, Republican of Florida and Carswell's original sponsor, and said, "If you want my opinion, he's a jackass"—but everyone expected Fong to vote for him.

Once again, one of the few people who did not share the general impression that Carswell was bound to be confirmed was Kennedy's young assistant Flug, and while the hearings were in progress he sent Kennedy another memorandum entitled "How to Beat Carswell," which began, "I smell blood. I think it can be done if we can get full civil-rights apparatus working, which it's beginning to do . . . [and show] his mediocrity, lack of candor before committee." The paper went on to lay out a head count of senators who could be expected to oppose Carswell because of his civil-rights record, along with those who might be persuaded to "go along with proper kinds of brotherly pressure"—forty-six in all. (This group was largely made up of moderates and liberals on both sides of the aisle— all of whom had voted against the Haynsworth nomination.) Those who could be expected to support Carswell, whatever the case against him, came to thirty-nine. (*This* group was largely made up of the Hruska-Eastland axis—right-wing Republicans from the North and right-wing Republicans and Democrats from the South; along with these were some moderates from both parties, including Southern Democrats who were not racists but who felt they had to go along with their racist constituents to get reëlected, and Northern Republicans who felt they had to support their President.) The remaining fifteen included "those who'd like to go along [with the anti-Carswell group] but have to overcome serious political problems" and "those who would be possibles." In conclusion, Flug wrote, "That means that to win we'd have to get five of the fifteen. . . . While it's a long shot, I don't think it's an impossibility." (Flug turned out to be wrong about three of the senators he thought were bound to oppose Carswell but also wrong about three he thought were bound to support him, so he came extraordinarily close to the final tally ten weeks later.)

The scent that Flug thought he detected was still quite faint, however, although an incident that occurred during the first day of the Carswell hearings had raised his hopes further. On that occasion Senator Kennedy asked Carswell for a list of all the clients he had represented in private practice who had later appeared before him in court. At this, Senator Griffin, the Minority Whip, angrily broke in and charged that the request was nothing more than "a fishing expedition." As Majority Whip, Kennedy was accustomed to jousting with Griffin on the floor of the Senate, but he found this rebuke offensive, for it suggested that he was trying to cast doubt, by innuendo, on the nominee's integrity. After the session, it was clear that Kennedy was smarting over the remark, and that led Flug to hope that he would now oppose the nomination actively, if only to show that his concern was serious. As Flug knew, it was one thing for a senator to make a speech and cast a vote against such a nomination, but it was quite another thing for him to work at defeating it. If Kennedy chose the latter course, his prestige as a member of the Democratic leadership and the facilities of his office, including Flug's time, would be a considerable boost to the opposition to Carswell.

"Griffin's attack gave us the impetus of irrationality to get through the next few weeks, when there wasn't any cohesive force against Carswell," Flug observed afterward. "It was important at that stage to have a little emotionalism."

By the time the hearings ended, on February 3rd, emotionalism was about all that Carswell's opponents had going for them. Only a handful of influential public figures had publicly come out against the nomination—George Meany, the head of the A.F.L.-C.I.O.; Senator William Proxmire, Democrat of Wisconsin (the first member of the Senate to take that position publicly); Senator Walter F. Mondale, Democrat of Minnesota (the second); and John Gardner, former Secretary of Health, Education, and Welfare and then director of the Urban Coalition. But two days after the hearings adjourned Senator Goodell unexpectedly took the floor of the Senate and denounced the nomination.

Everyone was surprised, and Mrs. Edelman was ecstatic at the news. "We had started going around to some senators— the usual Democratic stalwarts you can count on at times like that—and we got almost no response at all," she recalled not long ago. "One of the points they all made was that we couldn't win, or even come close, without Republican help, and everyone asked us how we could expect Republicans to go against their President twice in a row. Goodell's announcement was crucial, because it gave us a bipartisan start."

As for Goodell himself, he later explained his decision by pointing out that his vote against Judge Haynsworth had been based not on the conflict-of-interest charges against him, as the votes of most of that nominee's other opponents had been, but on his civil-rights and civil-liberties record. "Since Carswell was even worse on this score—and I read the hearings and many of his opinions—I had to vote against him," he went on. "Then, too, he seemed pedestrian as a judge in all areas of the law, especially in habeas-corpus cases." Although Goodell had not been subjected to much pressure before his announcement —as he observed, that was saved for senators who delayed their decisions—he was subjected to an unexpected and alarming amount of recrimination after it. "The same week that I came out against Carswell, I was the lead-off witness before the Foreign Relations Committee and strongly attacked the Administration on the war," he said. "That was a few weeks before the Republican Convention in New York State. Whether or not I would get the nomination was touch and go, and there were tremendous repercussions at the time over these positions of mine. That almost cut the baling wire holding my campaign together.

No one on either side had approached Goodell for his vote, but he had discussed the subject just before he announced

how he would vote in the course of a lunch meeting of the
Wednesday Club, which is a loosely knit group of a dozen
liberal and moderate Republican senators who meet most
Wednesdays in one or another of their offices for lunch and
political talk. The club, which ultimately was to be a subtle
but influential force in the fight over Carswell, had been
founded a few months earlier to provide a regular opportunity
for these senators to discuss common concerns, to alert each
other to political dangers they might be unaware of in current
or forthcoming legislation, and to create a more or less united
front on key issues, in the hope that the White House, which
ignored most of them individually, would listen to them col-
lectively.

"There is virtually no liaison between the White House and
these senators," George Mitrovich, Goodell's press secretary,
explained at the time. "The White House simply pays no
attention to them, while conservative senators have ready access and great influence there. No one from the White House
has come to, or even telephoned, our office in months. If the
President had these men over to the White House occasionally
or called now and then to get their opinions, he would create
an atmosphere that would make it difficult for them to oppose
him. It's utterly stupid not to do that. The President and
his staff simply don't understand the Senate—most of all, they
don't understand how seducible it is. As a result, they've
created a deep resentment among some of the younger Republicans here. There's a good bit of paranoia over in the
White House, particularly among the more partisan staff
people, and when these senators stand up to the President
his aides convince him that it's all politically motivated. Actually, there has rarely been an issue here that was more completely decided on its merits than the Carswell affair."

One member of the Wednesday Club was Marlow W. Cook, a freshman senator from Kentucky and a member of the Judiciary Committee, who had led the Administration's fight for Haynsworth, and who, it was generally assumed, would come out for Carswell, too, even if he did not actively participate in the contest. However, several people who attended the hearings noticed that while Cook bore down rather harshly on adverse witnesses during the early stages, he grew less and less willing to defend the nominee as more and more adverse testimony was given. Now, as the Wednesday Club members left the luncheon on February 4th, Cook took Goodell aside and told him that if he intended to come out against Carswell he would do well to look over the Judge's habeas-corpus rulings to support his stand. "I saw then that Marlow had doubts about the nominee's fitness," Goodell said later. "Of course, if he opposed Carswell after leading the fight for Haynsworth it would have a tremendous effect on other senators, especially other Republicans."

As it turned out, Cook did not publicly reveal his intentions until his name was called on the day of the vote, two months later. And many of his colleagues were as slow, or almost as slow, in revealing theirs. In the days before and after Goodell made his decision known, Mrs. Edelman and Verlin Nelson, of the A.D.A., her companion in this struggle almost from the start, visited several senators' offices to see where they stood on the nomination. The first stop was at the office of Senator Thomas F. Eagleton, a freshman Democrat from Missouri, who had opposed Haynsworth but had publicly stated that he was inclined to vote for Carswell. Since the Senator wasn't in—or so they were told—they left the scanty amount of material they had collected and went on to the office of Senator Alan Cranston, a freshman Democrat from California, where little interest was shown either in their appeal or in their material. From there, they went to the office of Senator Harold E. Hughes, a freshman Democrat from Iowa, one of whose aides told them that the Senator was considering making a statement against the nomination but hadn't enough facts to base it on. "We realized then that we needed some more material for these people," Nelson recalled afterward. "About this time, Brad Brasfield, of the U.A.W., joined us, and the three of us kind of stumbled along, getting stuff together and passing it out to anyone who showed any interest."

But even after they had compiled several more documents —including an impressive study of Carswell's civil-rights record on the bench, which was drawn up by Mrs. Edelman's assistant, Seymour, who had uncovered the golf-club incorporation papers—they had little more success in gaining recruits. At each office they went to, they were told, almost always by an aide, that the senator was reluctant to oppose another nomination unless there was more conclusive evidence than had been brought out so far to justify such a stand, and that, in any case, he wouldn't make a move so early. "Our reception was generally good, and it was clear that most of the people we saw wanted to go into the matter in depth," Nelson said later. "But the water looked cold, and nobody was willing to jump in."

Finally, Mrs. Edelman, Nelson, and Brasfield discussed the problem, and Mrs. Edelman suggested that with the combined forces represented they might bring Scott around if they threatened to oppose him during his fall election campaign. Since Scott had been reëlected in 1964—a disaster year for Republicans generally in the Goldwater debacle—partly through the dogged efforts of Clarence Mitchell, of the N.A.A.C.P., and his followers, who persuaded black voters in Pennsylvania to split their ticket and return Scott to the Senate as a reward for his twenty years of fighting for civil-rights progress, the threat that Mrs. Edelman proposed would have had great force.

But when word of the proposal reached Mitchell, who prided himself on his closeness to certain senators, especially influential senators like Scott, he was aghast at the suggestion.

"I won't be a party to anything that would harm my friend Senator Scott," he kept saying.

The others realized that Mitchell was primarily concerned at the time about the fate of the Voting Rights Act, which he had shepherded through Congress in 1965, and which he and Scott were now desperately trying to save from the Administration's attempts to weaken it. While Mrs. Edelman shared their concern on this score, she felt that the battle for the Voting Rights Act could be waged simultaneously with the battle against Carswell; both, she argued, involved the same principle, and both should be given the same attention.

With this in mind, Nelson and Brasfield went to one of Tydings' aides and asked to have a meeting with the Senator to discuss the possibility of his taking over the leadership of the move to defeat the nomination. Tydings wanted to know where Mitchell stood on the matter—since he had long been known on Capitol Hill as Mr. Civil Rights—and when word of the men's visit reached Mitchell it had a galvanizing effect. As a friend of Mitchell's said later, "Clarence had a temper tantrum when he heard about it. He rushed off to the Hill to talk to what he calls 'my senators.' If anybody is going to do anything about civil rights here, it's going to be Clarence." After some thirty years in Washington, Mitchell was as fussy about protocol as an ambassador's secretary, and he went down the line of liberal Democrats on the Judiciary Committee by seniority until he got to Tydings, who tentatively agreed to take over, although, as he later remarked, "there seemed depressingly little to take over."

Mitchell's commitment meant that there was far more to take over than there had been before. Without his help, Carswell's opponents would have had no hope; with it, they had

66

some. Despite his resentment over any interference in his province, his involvement in the Carswell case had been as early and as deep as anyone's. After the first meeting held in Bayh's office following the nomination, it was clear that he was close to tears. "But he saw he had zero support," one of the participants said later. "He kept trying to get others involved, but he became so emotional that they stopped listening. Still, he went on trying, and when things got moving his mood was decisive. In the end, it was Clarence more than anybody else who turned on the big guns in the labor movement."

Mitchell went at things with the single-minded intensity that had brought success to so many of the civil-rights battles he had fought over the years. "The most important thing I was troubled by in the beginning was that senators who had voted against Haynsworth and who were up for reëlection didn't want to take the political risk of voting against another nominee if there was no chance to win," he said afterward. "The big problem was how to convince them that there was a chance. For that, we needed time. Second, the White House had painted a picture of Carswell as a moderate and had succeeded in convincing people who ordinarily aren't likely to be taken in—men like Scott and Griffin—that it was a fair representation. We had to show them that he not only wasn't a moderate but wasn't even a conservative, that actually he was an outright reactionary. And, third, many senators felt that since they had rejected one nominee, they didn't want to overplay their role as advisers and consenters. We had to convince them that the safety of the nation was at stake."

As Rauh saw it at this stage, the most crucial need of all was time—first, so that further investigative work could be done to see if there were any more black marks on Carswell's record, and, second, so that a large enough grass-roots campaign against the nomination could be planted to convince members of the Senate that it would be riskier for them to vote for Carswell than against him. Once again, the Voting Rights Act was to play a crucial role. The previous December, the Senate had agreed to make the debate on the revision of the act its first order of business on the first day of business after March 1st. Now Carswell's foes saw a chance to buy a sizable chunk of time—at least a month—if they could delay the floor debates on the nomination until after that date.

This task fell to Tydings, and when the hearings ended and the Judiciary Committee went into executive session to consider the nomination, on February 3rd, he immediately moved that Carswell be called back to answer the charges that had been made since his appearance before the committee—chiefly those made by civil-rights lawyers who had testified about his treatment of them in court. Most of the committee's members were anxious to dispose of the nomination before it became any more embarrassing politically, and the motion lost by a vote of nine to six. In its place, a motion was approved to dispatch a letter to Carswell asking him to reply to the recent accusations in writing. (In his reply Carswell simply ignored the questions that had been raised and repeated his contention that he was not a racist.)

Then, in an unexpected move that appeared to undercut Tydings' efforts, Bayh, who was more optimistic about getting his direct-election amendment through than he was about defeating Carswell, tried to use the nomination to dislodge the amendment by calling for a package deal—a vote on Carswell in committee on February 9th, less than a week away, and a vote on direct election by April 24th. If Carswell's friends had accepted this motion, their man would almost certainly be on the Supreme Court today, since the time needed to build up resistance to the nomination would have been lost. But Senator Thurmond, who probably believed in Carswell more fervently than anyone else in the room, immediately and unwittingly set out to defeat the nomination. First, he moved that the Bayh proposal be tabled; since the other supporters of Carswell wanted to get the nomination to the floor for a vote, they turned down the Thurmond motion by a vote of twelve to four. That automatically made Bayh's proposal the pending order of business, whereupon Thurmond, having set a neat trap, jumped into it. To the delight of Carswell's foes and the dismay of his friends, Thurmond set off on a ranting filibuster, which went on until Eastland cut him off by adjourning the meeting, subject to reconvening at his call.

Tydings planned to use the committee's unique "right of holdover," a parliamentary device by which any member could ask for a one-week delay on any vote, which was granted automatically. His opponents were aware of this and hoped to force him to use the holdover before February 5th, for otherwise it would postpone a vote until February 12th, the beginning of the four-day recess for Lincoln's Birthday. To this end, they finally induced Thurmond to drop his filibuster when the committee met on February 4th by persuading him that it was harming Carswell far more than Bayh. Once the aid of this improbable ally was lost, Hart and Kennedy took over and let it be known that they would object to any committee meeting that day while the Senate was in session—another parliamentary device that is automatically granted on request. At this, Senator Eastland announced that he would wait until the Senate adjourned in the afternoon or evening and then reconvene the committee. Tydings thereupon threatened to keep the Senate in session all night if necessary—by way of a filibuster of his own—to stop the committee from meeting.

Outmaneuvered, Eastland and his allies gave up, and when the committee met on February 5th, Tydings used his right of holdover as expected. Before adjourning, the committee approved a revised version of Bayh's earlier proposal—to vote on Carswell on the first day after the Lincoln's Birthday recess, February 16th, and on the direct-election amendment by April 24th. With that, the committee debate came to a close.

Shortly afterward, Bayh left town to fulfill commitments he had made to speak at several colleges in southern California. Most of them were small places—junior and community colleges where surfing, rock music, and the latest in sports cars ordinarily took precedence over even the most pressing national concerns. To Bayh's surprise, he found that the students and faculty members at each school were deeply upset by the prospect of Judge Carswell's becoming Justice Carswell. To test the depth of this mood, Bayh began attacking the Presi-

dent's choice—in a region that was strong Nixon country, since
he was born and still spends much of his time there—and was
even more surprised by the strength of the favorable reaction
to each attack. In fact, he found that the stronger his attack
the stronger the response in favor of it, so, like any politician
who finds that something works, by the end of the tour Bayh
was throwing haymakers at Carswell with both arms.

"The audiences loved it," Keefe, who accompanied him on
the trip, said later. "I think that convinced him there was
grass-roots sentiment of great potential just waiting to be
used." That impression increased when Bayh stopped off, on
his way back to Washington, in Kansas City to address the
local bar association. He wanted to talk about direct election,
but his audience wanted to hear about Carswell, so he drew
on the arguments and rhetoric that had proved most effective
in California. The lawyers—a conservative lot, by and large—
listened attentively, applauded each time he made a telling
point, and gave him a standing ovation when he finished.

Although opposition outside the Senate was necessary, it wasn't sufficient, of course, without comparable opposition inside that body. As the days passed after the hearings ended, Mrs. Edelman and Nelson grew increasingly discouraged as they tramped from one senator's office to another only to be met by the same responses. The experience was so dispiriting that finally they left the Senate and went across the Capitol grounds to see what help they could get from members of the House. The first stop was at the office of Representative Don Edwards, Democrat of California, who was a leader of the Democratic Study Group, a loose collection of around a hundred and twenty liberal Democrats. The D.S.G. has often been of crucial influence in the House, and although that body has no say in executive nominations, Edwards felt that this one was of such importance to the nation that his group should do whatever it could to stop Carswell from reaching the Court. To this end, he immediately drafted a statement, got approval of other key members of the group over the telephone, and issued a press release while the two were still there.

Mrs. Edelman and Nelson then went to the office of Representative John Conyers, a Negro and a Democrat from Detroit, who had testified against the nomination at the hearings. Although they had little expectation that much would come from this meeting, they hoped that he might have some useful ideas, particularly about how they should go about preventing Minority Whip Griffin, who was also from Michigan, from going all out for Carswell, and how they might persuade Brooke, who was then still evaluating the situation, to break his silence. Conyers heard them out, and then, to their surprise, eagerly said, "Let's hold a meeting." He knew that Griffin could not hope to hold on to his leadership position if he opposed the nomination, but Conyers suspected that the Senator could at least be scared into working for Carswell out of the public view, which would at least limit his effectiveness. The meeting, which was attended by Mrs. Edelman, Nelson, Brasfield, and aides to the four Democratic senators involved, was largely devoted to a discussion of how the small anti-Carswell faction that existed could be broadened, how citizens' groups could be set up, and how the press could be sufficiently tempted by the case to do some more investigative work on its own.

Conyers turned out to be angrier about the nomination and more determined to fight it than anyone had expected. "I wanted to make it a precedent that any nominee to the Supreme Court who is a segregationist must automatically be rejected," he explained afterward. "When Carswell's name was sent to the Senate, everybody said, 'Let's be realistic and accept the fact that he can't be defeated.' I didn't share that view at all. You can't be an American who is trying to bring about reform in a place as resolutely archaic as Congress and think that way, because everything you do is unrealistic in ordinary terms. We had to fight. And we all saw that members of the House could bring pressure on members of the Senate —on men like Griffin and Brooke—and that this could be effective. Anyway, I knew that I couldn't walk away from it when I believed that Carswell was a terrible choice and that most senators didn't fully realize it."

One of the group's first efforts was to bring Brooke around, but at the start that looked hopeless. "Brooke was really bad," a man who worked on him from the outside said later. "He wouldn't even talk to us. Nobody could get through to him except Clarence Mitchell, and he was too sympathetic to push hard. When Brooke's staff learned what we wanted to talk about, they wouldn't let us in to see him. Finally, Roger Wilkins, Roy's nephew and formerly a high government official, got to Brooke's top aide, who told him that the Senator had been very impressed by a letter he had seen from a man who had been a shipmate of Carswell's in the Navy during the war and who said that Carswell had always been decent to the Negroes aboard. Why shouldn't he have been? In those days, the Navy was segregated and Negroes served mostly as messboys and cooks, and he had the same relationship to them as he'd had to his own family's servants back home— that is, treat your 'niggras' decently but keep them in their place. The letter was nonsense, and Brooke, who had been in a segregated unit in the Army, must have known it. Using it as a justification for not opposing Carswell made it look very much as if Brooke were trying to get off the hook." To impale him firmly on it, the group asked for support from black ministers and activists, along with sympathetic labor leaders, in Massachusetts, and as the mail, telegrams, telephone calls, and influential visitors began to arrive in great numbers in Brooke's office he gradually stopped talking about Carswell's shipmate.

On February 15th, Conyers released the text of an open letter he had written to Senator Griffin, which was reprinted by the tens of thousands and distributed throughout Michigan. Pointing out that the Senator had opposed Haynsworth because of the revelations about his financial conflicts of interest, Conyers demanded that Griffin now "speak out against the racism of Judge G. Harrold Carswell," went on to remind him that at the last N.A.A.C.P. banquet in Detroit he had allied himself with the aspirations of that group, and added, "I wonder what kind of remarks you are going to bring us this year." As it turned out, Griffin did not attend that banquet, but sent his regrets.

The day the letter was released, Conyers was at his home in Detroit when Stephen Schlossberg, general counsel for the U.A.W. and a leading participant in the movement to defeat Carswell almost from the start, telephoned him and said, "John, we've got to get ripping on this Carswell thing." Conyers agreed, and after a lengthy discussion the two men decided to set up an outfit called the Michigan Committee Against Racism in the Supreme Court—the first of the grass-roots lobbies against Carswell—in the hope that it would generate interest and help among influential citizens, concern on the part of the general public, and, finally, action by the press.

"We organized it practically overnight and put together a fantastic coalition," Conyers recalled afterward. The coalition included such disparate individuals and organizations as a district chairman of the Republican Party, a vice-president of the International Amalgamated Clothing Workers Union, the president of the Interdenominational Ministerial Alliance, the president of the Detroit chapter of the American Trial Lawyers' Association, the president of the Wolverine Bar Association, a member of the National Council of Catholic Women, and the executive director of the Metropolitan Detroit Jewish Community Council. Hundreds of thousands of broadsides headed "We Call on Senator Griffin to Oppose Carswell" were sent out, along with letters to members of the committee's component organizations urging them to "write, wire, or visit Senator Griffin in an effort to prevent the confirmation of G. Harrold Carswell."

Not long afterward, Conyers said, "Griffin was under such pressure at home that he wanted out. I understand he appealed to the White House to be released but was told that he couldn't back down on this one."

For Griffin's own part, he later claimed that while the campaign had hurt him badly in Michigan, he had not been cowed by it, and said, "I don't see how I could have worked any harder for Carswell." Others felt that he could have worked a lot harder if he had not found it necessary to work covertly in order to avoid letting his constituents in on what he was doing.

A couple of days after the Michigan committee had a sufficiently imposing number of sponsors, Conyers held a press conference in Washington to announce its formation. Reporters had to be cajoled into coming, since committees of one kind or another seem to be set up there every three or four minutes, and the bait was not the new group itself but, rather, the rumor that Senator Daniel K. Inouye, Democrat of Hawaii and Assistant Majority Whip, would appear to declare his intention to oppose the nomination. At the time, the campaign against Carswell had bogged down listlessly, and his opponents were desperate to get some news favorable to their side reported. As it happened, Inouye had let them know some time before that he would vote against confirmation, and they had asked him to hold off his announcement until a time when it would help most.

That time having arrived, Inouye told the reporters on hand

that the nominee was "at best mediocre and at worst a slap in the face of the judiciary," and added, "The only good thing I've heard about Judge Carswell is that the next nominee will be worse." The severity of this remark put it on television news broadcasts that night and on the front pages of many newspapers the next morning, and the importance of Inouye's leadership position all but assured that his stand would bring half a dozen other senators to the anti-Carswell side.

In the long run, few of the countless forces that pull and push at senators are stronger than the influence of their staffs. While influence is not the same as power, at times strong aides can make the two seem identical. To a great extent, the protracted and bitter quarrel over Judge Carswell's nomination to the Supreme Court was carried on by senatorial aides, and to an equally great extent the outcome was determined by their work. All this is not to say that any of them told their employers what to do, or even suggested a course of action openly; senators are far too vain and crotchety a lot for that. Also, experienced aides are aware that the consequences of a political decision for a politician are far different from what they are for someone who helps him reach it, and they are usually reluctant to press their man too hard. For the most part, staff members exert influence by carefully marshalling and presenting facts on both sides of an issue and by making sure that one side prevails. The most adroit of them also have an acute awareness of which direction their senator may be leaning in at any given moment and a sharp sense of timing. As the days and weeks passed, the efforts of assistants to the early leaders of the fight against the nomination had an increasing effect on their counterparts in other senators' offices, and these colleagues began to have an increasing effect on the senators *they* worked for.

A week after the hearings ended, Flug set off the first small explosion calculated to create this kind of chain reaction when he telephoned Thomas Bennett, legislative assistant to Senator Gaylord Nelson, Democrat of Wisconsin, and suggested that it might be a good idea to call a Monday Morning Meeting to talk abut Carswell. The Monday Morning Meeting—similar, on the staff level, to the Wednesday Club—consisted largely of liberal Democratic senators' legislative assistants, who discovered shortly after the 1968 election that the usual sources of information from the executive branch were closed off and decided that they could be of help to each other if they got together from time to time and discussed the major issues before the Senate.

Bennett agreed that it would be a good idea to call a meeting, and also agreed with Flug that it be billed as a frankly anti-Carswell session, to protect any aides who might not want to attend such an affair if it might seem to commit their senators to one side when they were uncommitted. Despite this, nearly thirty aides showed up for the meeting, which was held not on Monday but on Wednesday, February 4th, in a large room in the Old Senate Office Building that was otherwise used only on Tuesdays by senators' wives who gathered to roll bandages for the Red Cross. Rauh was on hand to present the case against Carswell, and in the opinion of several participants he was extremely persuasive. "Joe is a very passionate advocate, and by the time he was finished cutting up Carswell the Judge could have used the entire supply of bandages prepared by the ladies the day before," one of them said later. "Most of us had been unaware that a case of that magnitude could be made."

When Rauh completed his presentation, Flug got up and

went through the same head count that he had sent Kennedy. "That was dangerous, since no guy likes to be told how his boss is going to vote before his boss has voted," Flug said afterward. "But it worked, because after Rauh spoke and everybody saw that Carswell was a terrible choice and then the theoretical vote count showed he could be stopped, no one cared about a small matter like that. In fact, it was remarkable how little everybody cared throughout the fight about who got the credit, who was running things, or any of the other little sensibilities that often cripple this place."

In the opinion of some others who attended the meeting, its effect ranged from crucial to irrelevant. Probably the most balanced impression came from Bennett, who said later, "As a legislative assistant, you have such great demands on your time that you have to set priorities, and usually you set each one on the basis of how short a fuse a given issue has. Rauh presented his case so convincingly that it got those who were present to think about it seriously. Before that, they figured their bosses wouldn't go for it, but he exposed them to the basic facts—that Carswell was worse than Haynsworth, that the civil-rights people were dead set against him, and that he was not of the calibre to be on the Court. That got their attention and gave them information, and then Flug's head count, which may have seemed rather inflated at the time but still possible, made it look worthwhile. The upshot was that the meeting put Carswell on their agenda as a priority item."

Another participant, Douglas Jones, a former professor of economics who was legislative assistant to Senator Mike Gravel, Democrat of Alaska, found the affair helpful but by no means decisive. "My inclination toward Carswell was negative when I got to the meeting, but I hadn't made a judgment yet," he said later. "The main effect of the session was that it provided a bibliography of the material against Carswell. Then, gradually, the material I got afterward convinced me that my boss would probably want to oppose the nomination." Gravel was the only Northern Democrat to vote for Haynsworth, and it was generally assumed that he would also support Carswell. But no one, including Jones, had any idea of where he stood on the second nomination, because he had been out of town since it was announced. To prepare background information for him to read on his return, Jones obtained more material from Flug and then worked with other members of Gravel's staff to put it together.

"The principal question we faced was: If it is the right position, on the merits, to vote against Carswell, how does one go about marching, in a political sense, from a vote for Haynsworth to a vote against Carswell?" Jones explained. "We had to find a way to move logically from a yes vote to a no vote. We began by going over why the Senator had voted for Haynsworth. In that case, there had been three major concerns —judicial ethics, judicial stature, and the race issue. Senator Gravel felt at the time that while Haynsworth's sense of ethics could raise certain misgivings, they were not compelling enough to justify voting against him. On the question of judicial stature, the Senator felt that although Haynsworth was not the most eminent judge in the country, he was highly competent. As for the race issue, that seemed just not legitimate.

"Then we measured Carswell by these standards. In his case, the race issue clearly had been properly raised. And on ethics we felt that this includes a lot more than simply finances. For example, how does one use one's office? It was apparent from the hearings that Carswell's treatment of Northern lawyers working on voter registration was improper, and his behavior and demeanor in court suggested a lack of ethics in this sense.

After that, we had to consider the importance of Senator Gravel's having been the only Democrat from the North to support Haynsworth. If the Senator came out against Carswell, he would probably create a similar inclination among some other senators who had also voted for Haynsworth, because they would conclude that here was someone who had voted for Haynsworth, showing there was no sectional bias involved, but who just couldn't take Carswell. That meant Senator Gravel's vote would amount to several votes, not just one."

When Gravel returned to the capital, Jones gave him the memorandum the staff had prepared, along with a speech to accompany his announcement if it turned out that the Senator agreed with the staff's conclusions. Aside from these documents, there was little in the way of pressure on Gravel. During the entire seventy-nine days from the nomination to the final vote, his office received only seventy-five letters, postcards, and telegrams concerning Carswell—against him by a ratio of eight to one. To be sure, some union people phoned and stopped by, but they had little or no effect on him. Nor did the personal lobbying on the opposite side by Senator Ernest F. Hollings, Democrat of South Carolina, who took the opportunity offered by his daily association with Gravel as his jogging partner to ask him to support Carswell. In fact, the only effective appeal from the outside was a letter from Roy Wilkins, which Gravel found solidly persuasive.

Gravel spent most of his first weekend back in town going over the staff memorandum, the transcript of the hearings, Wilkins' letter, and a number of speeches made in the Senate during his absence. As Jones expected, the Senator found the evidence against Carswell so compelling that he decided he had to oppose the nomination, whatever the political implications. And, like a surprising number of other senators, he decided the issue solely on its merits. "This was one of those cases where most senators were statesmen," Jones remarked later. "In the privacy of the night, they thought about the Republic." While Gravel's decision was statesmanlike, the timing of his announcement was political. When Bayh and Kennedy learned that he was prepared to vote against the nomination, they got in touch with him and asked that he hold off making the statement on his stand until a propitious time. Gravel agreed and said that his speech was all ready.

On the day that the Senate recessed for Lincoln's Birthday, the Washington *Post* ran a long and minutely detailed editorial on Judge Carswell's civil-rights record—written by James Clayton, who was to compile a remarkable amount of original research for use in the battle against the nomination. After recounting, step by step, Carswell's judicial efforts to obstruct school desegregation in the South, Clayton concluded, "He proceeded as slowly with desegregation as any judge could without courting brutal rebuffs from above and even then he was reversed consistently. He refused to speed things up when higher courts and national policy required a speedup. He protested when the Fifth Circuit entered a specific order in a case going back to a judge who was known as an opponent of desegregation. This is a record of delay, postponement, resistance, almost all across the line." By this time, Herblock was directing his political cartoons against Carswell almost daily, and other political cartoonists and editorial writers across the country began joining the anti-Carswell forces in increasing numbers.

When the Judiciary Committee convened on February 16th to vote on the nomination, Carswell's opponents had no expectation that he would be defeated in the committee, but they had some hope that the division would be narrow enough to impress any senators who might still be undecided when the time came for a final vote on the Senate floor. This hope rested mainly on the uncertainty about which way Republican Senators Cook and Mathias, along with Quentin N. Burdick, Democrat of North Dakota, might go, since all of them had privately expressed misgivings about the nominee. But in the end all three went with the majority, making the tally thirteen to four. The first vote, that morning, was twelve to four, with Cook abstaining. He had twenty-four hours to make up his mind, which he did by that afternoon. Still, his few hours of hesitation encouraged Bayh and the other dissenters about the prospect of bringing Cook around before the final vote.

The hearing record was published that day, and Rauh was surprised to find that although it had been officially closed by the chairman at the end of the hearings, except for the addition of Carswell's letter, it now included a twenty-four-page letter from Hruska purporting to answer Rauh's testimony on the final day. When Rauh read the letter, he saw why Eastland had not permitted him an opportunity to offer a surrebuttal, for the document, which had been prepared by the Justice Department and revised in Hruska's office, was a concoction of inaccuracies and half truths. However, Rauh was greatly cheered when he noticed that Hruska alone had signed the letter, whereas in similar circumstances in the Haynsworth case he had signed a joint letter with Senator Cook. "When I saw that, I gave a whoop, because it meant that Cook was still loose," Rauh said later. "So there was hope after all." That hope rose a couple of days later after Cook told reporters that despite his vote in the committee, he intended to "reserve decision" on the final vote when the nomination reached the floor.

Under an agreement reached by members of the Judiciary Committee, the minority report on the hearings was to be filed ten days after the majority view was submitted. To start the clock running, Hruska submitted it the day the committee voted out the nomination. Bayh and the three other opponents were slightly encouraged to see that Cook hadn't signed the document and that Mathias and Burdick had filed separate views expressing some reservations about the nominee. But the four were discouraged by the speed with which Hruska had acted, for it meant that the debate on the nomination would reach the Senate floor on the morning of February 27th —that is, in front of, not behind, the Voting Rights Act. On the following day, though, Senator Mike Mansfield, of Montana, the Majority Leader, announced that the nomination probably would not be brought to the floor until after the Voting Rights Act was disposed of. This made it clear that he intended to use the nomination as a procedural device to expedite passage of the Voting Rights Act. If the act reached the floor first, its opponents would not try to filibuster it to death, as they otherwise would have, because they did not want to delay the vote on Carswell.

By this time, it also appeared that Mansfield had begun to see that the forces lining up against the nominee were not as feeble as he had thought. One day during this period, Charles Ferris, general counsel for the Senate Democratic Policy Committee, ran into Flug and asked how his cause was shaping up. Flug said he thought they had forty-four votes, and when Ferris laughed at the claim Flug pulled out the tally sheet he always carried with him and went down the list. Unable to find anything wrong with the count, Ferris sobered at once. Later, he reported this encounter to Mansfield, who also seemed impressed.

Although liberals outnumber conservatives in the Senate, ordinarily conservatives are far more effective, largely because they are more willing to paper over their differences for the sake of unity, whereas liberals insist on emphasizing the palest shades of difference in their various positions to demonstrate for the record that they are thinking for themselves. By February 20th, the four dissenters' aides had completed a draft of the minority report on the hearings. To heighten its impact, they put it in the simplest form—a brief introduction stating that while the signatories opposed the nomination for varying reasons, they agree on the major points, which then followed. The draft was submitted to the four senators that day, and their liberalism soon emerged.

"Late that afternoon, everything fell apart," one of the authors said later. "It was a circus. The Senate was still in session, and the four got together just off the floor to go over the draft. They all refused to sign it unless it was rewritten as they wanted, and they all wanted something different. One of them wanted to play up this point and play down another, while the second wanted to do the reverse, the third wanted to emphasize something entirely different, and the fourth was dissatisfied with the whole thing. Also, the report was very tough and very purple, since it was a first draft, but apparently they thought it was the final version. They realized they would be signing a very strong document without sufficient evidence —for instance, on the subject of Carswell's evasiveness before the committee, which hadn't been corroborated yet—and they just refused."

The impasse seemed unbreakable and, to the report's authors, a disaster from just about every point of view. To begin with, they knew that if the four senators didn't sign the same report, there would be no chance of getting other senators to line up with an obviously fragmented opposition. Moreover, without a cohesive report signed by all four, they couldn't hope to persuade outsiders to lobby against the nomination. Members of the press were watching closely, too, and if a weak and inconclusive report convinced them that the effort was not serious and united, they would stop covering the story. And, finally, Mansfield was the key man, and if he concluded that the four senators were squabbling among themselves rather than working tightly together for maximum effect, he wouldn't bother helping them out in all the large and small ways open to him as Majority Leader.

To avert these calamities, two of the aides revised the report, excising the more inflammatory prose and unsubstantiated points, like the matter of Carswell's candor before the committee. That done, they presented the result—a pale document by any measure—and after Kennedy spent an hour and a half persuading the others to accept the document they finally signed it, late on the afternoon of February 26th, the deadline for its submission. "We had hoped for a really stinging report that would catch the attention of other senators and the press and create a rallying point for the opposition," one of the aides said later. "The final version was about as stinging as oatmeal, but at least it concealed the division within our ranks. That helped."

Another bit of help turned up the next day, in the form of a *Times* story describing in detail how shortly after Carswell became a U.S. Attorney he helped organize the Seminole Boosters, an all-white club set up to raise funds for the Florida State University's athletic program. "The story wasn't a big one, but it kept things alive," Flug said later. "A lot of senators were scared by then that there would be a real bombshell, and the Boosters kept them scared. That stopped many of them from coming out for Carswell early and locking themselves in." While the possibility of a bombshell may have stopped some members of the Senate from announcing their support for Carswell, it did not prompt any of them to announce their opposition. Five weeks after the nomination was made, only nineteen senators had come out against it. Of these, only three were Republicans—Goodell, Brooke, and Jacob Javits, of New York (who held off until after the New York *Post* had editorially chased him around the block several times and Brooke had made his speech).

Few lines of work make one less disposed to defy established authority than the law. When that authority is the President of the United States and the issue involves his basic policy and his personal prestige, only a lawyer who is uncommonly relaxed about the opinions of his colleagues and his fellow-citizens, about his relations with his clients, including those with cases before the government, and about the state of his tax returns would ordinarily be eager to stand up to him openly. Yet President Nixon's nomination of Carswell ultimately brought lawyers rallying by the thousands—from Wall Street, from law schools, from large cities and small towns across the country, and from within the Administration itself— to challenge the President. Only a handful of lawyers had publicly come out against the Haynsworth nomination—most of them comparatively secure professors of law—apparently because the case against him concerned not his legal qualifications but his sense of ethics, which was not enough to arouse members of the legal profession sufficiently for them to risk open opposition.

But now, as the case against Carswell began to clearly demonstrate his dismal record in the field of human and civil rights and his lack of judicial stature in general, even lawyers who had cautiously avoided any kind of public controversy throughout their professional lives set out to do what they could, both publicly and privately, to defeat the nomination. The first sign of this emerged during the last week in February, when a small group of some of New York's most eminent lawyers decided that they had to act immediately if Carswell was to be stopped from taking the seat once occupied by Justice Oliver Wendell Holmes. Led by Samuel I. Rosenman, a speechwriter for President Franklin Roosevelt and a former president of the New York City Bar Association, the group was made up of Bethuel M. Webster, another former president of that bar association; Francis T. P. Plimpton, the current president; and Bruce Bromley, a former judge of the New York Court of Appeals and now a leading Wall Street lawyer.

"We were stunned when we learned what they wanted to do," Bayh's assistant P. J. Mode said later. "About the last thing we expected was that men who were so much a part of the Establishment—in fact, they *are* the legal establishment— would be willing to attack a Supreme Court nominee without any prodding from anyone."

Rauh was surprised, too. "Men like these are generally moderates, but most of the time they avoid getting embroiled in such affairs, and their acquiescence ultimately gives support to the conservatives," he explained. "Now they apparently saw that they couldn't stand by any longer if moderation—not to mention the system—was going to be preserved in this country."

Bayh immediately recognized the great potential in even a small group like this one, and on his instructions Mode quickly got in touch with the four. When he learned that they planned to sign a letter urging Carswell's defeat in the Senate and place it as a full-page advertisement in the country's largest newspapers, he suggested that it would be far more effective if they persuaded other leading attorneys to sign the letter, too. It was a small start, but in time it was to produce immense results.

Although at this stage Bayh had still not made his decision to take active leadership of the anti-Carswell movement, his staff realized that he was days, or perhaps hours, from it. In anticipation of this step, Keefe, Bayh's chief aide, met with Mrs. Edelman, Nelson, and Brasfield on the day the minority report was filed to go over what they had been doing and to give them whatever help and encouragement he could. Above all, they needed encouragement. "Despite all of our work, we still had only nineteen firm votes," Mrs. Edelman recalled not long ago. "It just killed us."

The three had set up a small office—with the space supplied by the A.D.A., a clerk and a secretary by a private lawyer who was concerned about the nomination, and the postage by the U.A.W.—and had prepared the first of what they hoped would be an increasingly impressive series of broadsides called "Facts on the Nomination." The three also reported that they had some studies of Carswell's judicial history almost ready for distribution, and Mrs. Edelman added that she had been getting in touch with friends and acquaintances who taught at law schools in the East and urging them to turn on whatever pressure they could to persuade uncommitted senators from their states to commit themselves to the anti-Carswell cause. Most important, the group told Keefe of their efforts to get mail campaigns going in various key states, and said that they hoped the unions and the civil-rights groups, which had networks for that kind of operation, would take over.

"Mail was very, very important," Mrs. Edelman explained later. "For example, Senator Eagleton was inclined to come out for Carswell quite early. I heard that his staff was pressing him to turn around but that he wasn't getting any mail and wouldn't listen. So we went to work, and when I ran into him at a dinner party several weeks later he told me that the mail in his office was running three to one against Carswell and was voluminous. I asked him where he stood, and he said that while he wasn't going to make it public just then, I didn't have to worry. So we added him to our head count."

The same day that Mrs. Edelman and her two associates met with Keefe, Congressman Conyers held another meeting—the largest so far, with Senate staff members, several Democratic members of the House, and the usual group of outsiders—to devise the next moves. The chief problem was how they might line up more state and local outfits to work against the nomination, and after some discussion the standard list of labor, civil-rights, and civic organizations was drawn up and parcelled out among the participants. Conyers asked his House colleagues to do what they could to generate opposition to the nomination in their districts among professional—particularly legal—groups and civic organizations. (Not long afterward, Representative Abner Mikva, of Illinois, persuaded seventy Chicago lawyers to sign a telegram opposing Carswell, and Representative William F. Ryan, of New York, helped persuade the city bar association to pass a resolution calling for defeat of the nomination.) And everyone agreed to do what he could to get the press, which so far had had little to say against Carswell, involved and working in investigations of his background and his record.

Then someone suggested that more should be done in the way of getting help from law schools around the country to broaden Mrs. Edelman's efforts. Conyers promised to appeal to the deans of the four leading law schools in Michigan. (Ultimately, he lined up all four of them.) As it happened, Professor Lowenthal, who had testified at the hearings, had called Mazaroff in Tydings' office just a couple of days earlier to ask what more he could do to help. He had already done a great amount of work by enlisting the support of law-school deans and professors to defeat the nomination. Mazaroff suggested that he serve as liaison between the Rosenman group and the Senate, and told him that the group planned to hold a large press conference as soon as they had enough signatures on their letter to make an impressive showing; they also intended to bring along Dean Derek Bok, of the Harvard Law School, Dean Louis Pollak, of the Yale Law School, and Dean-elect Bernard Wolfman, of the University of Pennsylvania Law School, who would be ready to discuss the nomination with any senators who wanted to hear their side, and Mazaroff asked Lowenthal to coördinate this effort, too. Mazaroff had mentioned this conversation to Lee Miller, another Tydings aide, who now reported it to those attending the Conyers meeting, and they agreed that Lowenthal would be the ideal man to oversee the contacts made with the legal academic community.

Before Carswell's nomination, most members of the Senate apparently felt that a Supreme Court nominee's political philosophy was his own, and the President's, business, and that they had no right to include it in their considerations of whether a man should be confirmed. A number of them changed their minds when their attention was called to an article in the March issue of the *Yale Law Journal* entitled "A Note on Senatorial Consideration of Supreme Court Nominees." Its author, Professor Charles L. Black, Jr., emphatically disagreed with the prevailing opinion. "If a President should desire, and if chance should give him the opportunity, to change entirely the character of the Supreme Court, shaping it after his own political image, nothing would stand in his way except the United States Senate," he began the article. "Few Constitutional questions are, then, of more moment than the question whether a senator properly may, or even at some times in duty must, vote against a nominee to that Court, on the ground that the nominee holds views which, when transposed into judicial decisions, are likely, in the senator's judgment, to be very bad for the country."

If one argued that senators had no such right, Black went on, then one gave the President a power disproportionate to what the Founding Fathers had intended. Early in the Constitutional Convention, he explained, the participants agreed to give the Senate the exclusive power to appoint all judges, and not until later was the President given any role in the process, which, Black wrote, "must have meant that those who wanted appointment by the Senate alone . . . were satisfied that a compromise had been reached, and did not think the legislative part in the process had been reduced to the minimum." In "The Federalist," he continued, Hamilton had observed that the Senate's veto power over any selection "would be an excellent check upon a spirit of favoritism in the President, and would tend greatly to prevent the appointment of unfit characters from state prejudice, from family connection, from personal attachment, or from a view to popularity." Moreover, Black asserted, "In a world that knows that a man's social philosophy shapes his judicial behavior, that philosophy is a factor in his fitness. If it is a philosophy the senator thinks will make a judge whose service on the bench will hurt the country, then the senator can do right only by treating this judgment of his, unencumbered by deference to the President's, as a satisfactory basis in itself for a negative vote."

Black's article was distributed among members of the Senate who were uncommitted or were believed to be having doubts about the nominee's fitness for the highest court. Some of them were sufficiently impressed to go back to studies of what those who attended the Constitutional Convention had in mind when they gave the President the power to nominate and the Senate the power to accept or reject a nomination. Senator Richard S. Schweiker, a freshman Republican from Pennsylvania, who was to play a key role at the end of the contest over Carswell's nomination, was greatly influenced by these documents.

Schweiker had come out for Carswell immediately after

95

Hruska's briefing on the day of the nomination, and everyone assumed that he would stick to his decision—chiefly because of his relationship to Senator Scott, his senior colleague from Pennsylvania. As Minority Leader, Scott would be subject to attack within the Senate by those who wanted his job if he couldn't keep even his own junior colleague in line. And since Scott was up for reëlection, a defection on Schweiker's part would open Scott's flank to attack from outside the Senate by liberals and moderates back home, who would be sure to point out that the case against Carswell was so compelling that even a freshman senator who had every reason, politically speaking, to vote as Scott did couldn't bring himself to. And, finally, Schweiker hoped to wipe out the effect of his votes against the A.B.M. and Haynsworth, both of which the Administration and conservatives back home deeply resented.

"I wanted to vote for Carswell, and at first I decided that the charges against him were more political than real," Schweiker said later. "But after reading Black's article and the studies on the Constitutional Convention and seeing what the Founding Fathers intended, I concluded that my first decision had been based on a misunderstanding of the Constitution. Having already made a mistake, I didn't want to repeat it. I literally forced myself not to get fixed in an inflexible position. Then, the deeper I got into the facts, the more I realized, first, that I had a terrific responsibility and hadn't been fully aware of the Constitutional aspects of it. Second, I realized that Hruska's assertion about Carswell's being highly qualified was untrue. And, third, I realized that with human rights making up such a crucial part of our problems today and his having been reversed unanimously seventeen times in that area, he just wasn't a man for our time."

The Hruska-Eastland camp still had two days—Friday, February 27th, and Saturday, February 28th—in which to push the nomination onto the floor ahead of the Voting Rights Act, but Mansfield announced that any request to postpone floor action on the nomination for a day would be honored, as tradition dictated, and that no session would be held on Saturday except by unanimous consent. Since Bayh and his allies were prepared to request postponement and object to a Saturday session, that held off the debate until March 1st, when the Voting Rights Act became the first order of business.

Senators Scott and Hart had drafted and co-sponsored a compromise revision of that law designed to deflect the Administration's efforts to weaken it, and they were confident that the Southerners who opposed the act would be forced to see that a delay on the compromise bill would mean a delay on the Carswell nomination. Since the Southerners did not have the votes to defeat the compromise, it was assumed that they would reluctantly accept action on it so that they could get on to confirming their nominee. Also, Easter came early that year, with the recess for it beginning on March 27th, and since the Senate had to get through the debate on the act and then

97

the debate on the nomination before Carswell could come up for a final vote, it was clear that a delay of even a couple of days might postpone that vote until early April.

At the outset, Carswell's opponents had hoped for a month more to build up opposition, and Thurmond had given it to them when he filibustered against the direct-election amendment in the Judiciary Committee. Another month was desperately needed, but no one had much hope of gaining it until Senator James B. Allen, a freshman Democrat from Alabama and the Senate's leading redneck, rose and began filibustering against the Voting Rights Act—not with any hope of defeating it but merely to show the voters back home that he had tried. In the end, that gave the anti-Carswell forces slightly more than another month. (When it was all over, Senator Tydings asked, "You know who defeated Carswell?" and he answered, "Thurmond and Allen.")

On March 2nd, an Associated Press poll showed that thirty-seven senators were for Carswell, with eight more leaning that way. According to the poll, the number of opponents was twenty. Discouraging as this was, the opposition doggedly pressed on. (Its members would have taken great comfort if the A.P. had picked up a story that was published the next day in the Atlanta *Constitution* revealing Judge Tuttle's withdrawal of his offer to testify at the hearings on Carswell's behalf. United Press International also missed it, so the account didn't reach Northern newspapers or the Bayh group. However, it apparently reached Carswell's friends in the Senate, for senators who had repeated, day after day, the importance of Carswell's having the firm support of eminent jurists like Tuttle suddenly stopped mentioning it on the day the story appeared in the *Constitution* and never brought up the subject again.)

About this time, the work done by Mrs. Edelman and Professor Lowenthal began to produce results, as twenty-five professors at the U.C.L.A. Law School and nineteen professors at the University of Virginia Law School, the academic home of the Southern aristocracy, signed formal protests against the nomination. And then Senator Robert W. Packwood, a freshman Republican from Oregon, who was widely expected to back Carswell, privately told Bayh that he would oppose the nominee. Packwood also told Bayh that he did not want his decision revealed, because he hoped to avoid the kind of arm-twisting he had suffered after letting the White House know that he meant to vote against Haynsworth. In that fight, the Administration had openly threatened members of its own party with reprisals if they opposed Haynsworth—strong opponents in their next primary campaigns; cutoffs or slowdowns of funds for dams, bridges, and patronage; and complete loss of access to the President or anyone else in the White House. That strategy had backfired deafeningly. For instance, when a high official of the Department of Agriculture called a Midwestern senator and warned him that agricultural subsidies to his state would be cut back if he opposed Haynsworth, the senator, who was ready to back Shirley Temple if the President named her to the Court, became so angry that he voted against Haynsworth.

Members of the White House staff learned from this kind of experience that bullying didn't always work, and when it came to Carswell they relied—until nearly the end, anyway—on polite inquiries about where a given senator stood and on quiet persuasion when they found that he was uncertain or had decided to vote against them. While participants in the contest later attributed Carswell's downfall to a variety of causes—Thurmond's and Allen's filibusters, the work done by

Mrs. Edelman and other outsiders, the influence of the legal community, Hruska's clumsiness, the effect of Senate aides—perhaps the central cause was the White House staff's flailing incompetence.

As a number of Republican senators observed afterward, the only thing that was worse than the White House's lack of courtesy toward the Senate was its bumbling intelligence system. Packwood, for example, had learned from the Haynsworth case that the staff there couldn't be trusted even in the most elementary ways. When he let the White House know that he meant to oppose it then, he was asked to at least not announce his intention so that other Republicans wouldn't be influenced by his decision, as is often the case when senators have similar constituencies and backgrounds. Packwood agreed to that, and he also agreed to be accommodating when the time for the vote came and he was summoned off the floor by a telephone call from a White House aide who breathlessly told him that the result was going to be very close and asked him to hold back his vote on the first roll call to make the margin look even narrower, which might persuade others that a bandwagon was on its way and that they had better clamber aboard. To Packwood's bitter embarrassment, the bandwagon turned out to be rolling off in the opposite direction, for without his vote the final tally was fifty-four to forty-five against the nomination, which made him look not only like an opportunist but like an opportunist who couldn't count.

In any event, the Bayh-Brooke forces considered the White House their staunchest ally in the fight over Carswell, and this appraisal was concurred in by most Republican senators, ranging from conservatives to liberals. For instance, after the fight Senator Robert Dole, a conservative Republican from Kansas, who fought hard for Carswell, described the White House aides as "those idiots downtown."

By the time the floor debate on the nomination got under way, a group of students at the Columbia University Law School had spent several weeks compiling a collection of Judge Carswell's published decisions (mostly from the *Federal Supplement*, which includes only those decisions that federal District Court judges themselves submit for publication), on the off chance that they would find compelling enough evidence in the Judge's rate of reversals by higher courts to persuade undecided members of the Senate to decide against him. John Adler, an associate of a prominent Wall Street law firm, had learned about their work and had put them in touch with the Ripon Society, a liberal Republican group that had offered to serve as their publicity outlet if they came up with anything startling. As it turned out, the results of the students' compilation were so stunning that the Ripon Society called a press conference in Washington on March 5th, at which it revealed that of Carswell's eighty-four published decisions nearly sixty per cent had been reversed, or more than twice the average rate of the other judges in the Fifth Circuit District Courts.

That produced headlines around the country, and Attorney General Mitchell immediately responded with the charge that published decisions constituted only a small part of the total and were obviously an invalid measure. The Columbia students challenged him to withdraw the nomination if an examination of *all* Judge Carswell's decisions showed that he fell below a percentile to be chosen by Mitchell. Mitchell ignored the challenge. The students went ahead anyway, and completed a monumental study—covering some fifteen thousand cases—which showed that Carswell had been reversed more than forty per cent of the time, or one-third more often than the average of all his fellow-judges; of the sixty-seven judges in that circuit, only six had worse records. More or less in passing, the study also revealed that the longer Carswell had been on the bench, the more often he had been reversed. All this demonstrated that whatever else Judge Carswell was, he was not the "strict constructionist" of the Constitution that President Nixon claimed him to be.

On the morning of March 10th, the day that Bayh instructed his staff to crank up for an all-out fight against the nomination, another debate over who was going to lead the opposition was just being resolved in another Senate office. Tydings' aides had been urging him to assume this role for some time, and at almost the same hour that Bayh finally decided to take it over Tydings did, too. Exultant, his aides set out to arrange a meeting Tydings wanted called, to be attended by Senators Bayh, Kennedy, Hart, Brooke, and Javits, along with their aides, and by Rauh, Clarence Mitchell, and a couple of labor lobbyists, with Tydings as chairman. In the meantime, however, another of Tydings' staff men convinced him that an even more important occasion than the vote on Carswell would be the upcoming election in November, and persuaded the Senator to hold a press conference as soon as he could in Baltimore, where he was expected to run rather poorly, on a pressing local matter. Half an hour before the anti-Carswell group was to meet, in Room 207, just off the Senate floor, Tydings decided that it was vital for him to go to Baltimore, and left.

The aides who had called the meeting in his name were disappointed at his departure, but they finally collected themselves as the other participants gathered outside the conference room, and tried to edge Hart inside first, in the hope that he would then take the chair and inherit the leadership. Hart's aide saw what they were up to, and edged the Senator away from them. The two aides then moved toward Kennedy, whose aide moved him away, too. Finally, the whole group entered the room willy-nilly, and one of Tydings' men, grasping for a way out of the debacle, took the floor and explained some of the problems involved in such a fight. Since everyone there knew the problems as well as or better than he did, he quickly fell into an embarrassed silence. No one spoke for a long time, and it appeared that the meeting was about to collapse, when Bayh suggested that it might be helpful to form two teams, one headed by a couple of Democrats and one by a couple of Republicans. He added that he would be willing to serve as one of the Democrats, whereupon a Tydings man suggested his boss as the other. Then Brooke said that, of course, he would take one of the Republican posts, and Javits agreed to take the fourth slot. That settled, they discussed which senators might be called on to make lengthy speeches to hold the floor, and what strategy should be followed to insure that the opposition didn't outmaneuver them and call for a vote before they were ready. When the meeting broke up, it was tacitly agreed all around that Bayh would be the leader.

As it happened, Bayh and his aides were unaware that any question of leadership was involved, and they had already begun to scout for senators who would take part in the debate, which was expected to begin in a couple of days, and help hold off the pro-Carswell forces until after the Easter recess. Bayh had asked a couple of his aides to prepare a speech for him to deliver, and to "get plugged in" to such outside groups as the Leadership Conference, the A.D.A., labor unions, and any organizations that might help them do the necessary legal research on Carswell's record.

"We soon learned that one of our biggest problems was bum dope—unfounded rumors and misleading tips," Mode recalled later. "We got a lot of these, and had to chase down every one. Obviously, the other side could have blown us out of the water if they caught us making a false charge. At the same time, the pressure on us to come up with something new was terrific. Reporters had to be fed new material constantly to keep interest alive. And staff guys from other senators' offices kept begging for that one thing that would bring their wavering bosses around."

According to an outside lawyer who came to Bayh's office with what he believed was evidence that Carswell had been involved in a financial project of a questionable nature, the lack of legal help available there was shocking. "I had expected cubicle after cubicle filled with lawyers equipped with fine-tooth combs when I went to Bayh's suite," he said later. "But all they had was one lawyer working on this incredibly complicated stuff, and even he wasn't on it full time."

Actually, his expectations were unreasonable, for most senators do not have the funds, the staff, or even the space to conduct such investigations. To make up for this, Wise, Bayh's press officer, who had been a Washington correspondent for *Life* before moving to the Hill, set out to get the press interested in the story. "National magazines like *Life*, *Time*, and *Newsweek*, along with big-city newspapers and TV networks, have enormous resources—far more than a U.S. senator can command—and I knew from my experience as a reporter that they can often be persuaded to act as a senator's investigative arm if the story looks big," he explained recently. "So I arranged to give them all the tips we got, and they ran down ten blind alleys for every payoff." Wise also kept in daily, and sometimes hourly, touch with television and radio networks, keeping them slightly ahead of the game so they would be prepared if something new broke.

The day after Bayh took over as leader of the small band of senators who had declared their opposition to the nomination—only twenty-two in all, including himself—a petition was released bearing the signatures of over five hundred professional men and women from ten government departments and agencies who called on the Senate to reject Carswell because of his "utter lack of qualifications as a jurist." It is not at all uncommon for members of the executive branch to covertly undermine the President they supposedly serve, but it is exceedingly uncommon for them to undermine him openly—especially in the case of President Nixon, who has been known for his swift reprisals against dissension in the ranks.

Later the same day, Rosenman, Plimpton, Webster, and Bromley, accompanied by the deans of the Harvard, Yale, and University of Pennsylvania Law Schools, held a large press conference in Washington and released the text of an open letter appealing to members of the Senate to reject the nomination. As originally planned, the letter was to be published as a full-page advertisement in the country's major newspapers; acting on Mode's earlier suggestion, the four principal signatories had got the document signed by three hundred and fifty lawyers, including some of the nation's most distinguished judges, law professors, heads of bar associations, former high government officials, and private attorneys.

"The outpouring of sentiment against Carswell from men in the highest positions in the legal world was astonishing," Bayh said later. "And it was most effective." One effect was that it stopped Carswell's backers from claiming, in the words of one of them, that the opposition was made up entirely of

"South-haters, knee-jerk liberals, and Nixon-baiters." But a far more important effect was that the stand taken by these lawyers encouraged others to join them; within a few days, a hundred more had signed the letter, and additional hundreds of lawyers around the country began working locally to drum up opposition to the nomination.

When the press conference broke up, the three deans went off to meet with a dozen or so senators, from both sides of the aisle, who either hadn't made up their minds or had decided to oppose Carswell and felt they needed additional arguments to justify their votes. Senator Schweiker spent nearly an hour with the three, and listened attentively as they went over Carswell's judicial record in detail—the kinds of reversals he had had, his lack of scholarly work, the poor quality of his opinions, and the lack of respect shown for him by many of his peers. Afterward, Schweiker said that he had been deeply impressed by these arguments. His reaction was encouraging, but the very short roster of Republican senators opposing Carswell was becoming more and more discouraging to Bayh and his colleagues. Although Flug still held to his count of forty-four votes against the nominee, Bayh's staff put it at only forty, which meant that if all one hundred senators were present eleven more votes would be needed—most, or perhaps all, of them from Republicans; at the time, only Goodell, Brooke, Javits, and Packwood were committed to the opposition. To persuade others to join them, Bayh prevailed on Senator Clifford P. Case, Republican of New Jersey and one of the leading members of his party in the Senate, to announce his decision to oppose Carswell on the day that the Rosenman letter was released. It was hoped that Case's prestige would help convince other Republicans—mainly men like Schweiker and Mathias, who were leaning in the same direction—that the only honorable course was to follow him.

Another event of great significance occurred that day when an assistant in Tydings' office who was going through the mail came upon a letter from Atlanta containing a clipping of the *Constitution* story about Judge Tuttle's withdrawal of his offer to testify on Carswell's behalf. This was rushed to Tydings, and he telephoned Tuttle, who confirmed the report but, for the time, refused to make his position known publicly. The next morning, Tydings' aide Miller took a copy of the article to a strategy meeting in Bayh's office, and the participants discussed whether this might be the "one more thing" that so many senators were waiting for to justify a vote against Carswell. But since Tuttle refused to confirm the story, no one could figure out what use it might be put to. After the meeting broke up, Flug returned to his office to find a telephone call waiting from Joseph Kraft, the Washington *Post* columnist, who asked if anything new had turned up. Flug told him about the clipping and suggested that he call the *Constitution* to see if he could get more information on the story.

Late on the afternoon of March 13th, the Senate passed the amended Voting Rights Act, and the nomination of Judge Carswell became the pending order of business. Since the time for adjournment was near, little of significance happened in the way of debate. What was of great significance, though, was that Scott repeated his endorsement of the nominee and Griffin announced his—both with obvious reluctance, to be sure, but still with the assurance that they meant to stand by the President's choice.

Some of Carswell's opponents in the Senate had hoped that the record built up against him since he was named would persuade both men to refuse to support him, but that hope was more fond than real, for it was clear that neither could take such a stand and hope to retain his leadership post. However, both of them were angry at the way the Administration had failed to warn them at the start about the kind of opposition from civil-rights and labor groups that was bound to arise. After Scott reconfirmed his position, one of his Republican colleagues shook his head and muttered, "Hugh just committed political suicide." But others maintained that it was a case of political homicide, committed by the White House.

On the morning of the first full day of debate on the nomination—Monday, March 16th—Kraft's column in the *Post* recounted the story of how Judge Tuttle had telephoned Carswell and withdrawn his offer to testify for him at the hearings. By that time, Tydings had finally prevailed on Tuttle to confirm the story, and had received a telegram to that effect over the weekend. Apparently, Carswell's friends in the Senate learned of this and put counterpressure on Tuttle, for he sent Tydings two more telegrams, each weaker than the one before. Even so, the substance of the final wire was that he had withdrawn his support and had told Carswell so. On Tuesday, Tydings inserted the telegrams in the record during the floor debate, over the frantic protests of Hruska, who argued that Tuttle hadn't withdrawn his endorsement but had merely been unwilling to state it publicly. Griffin, for one, refused to join in this futile exercise, and told reporters, "It doesn't help when a respected jurist like Tuttle withdraws his support."

This blow to Carswell's chances sent Hruska reeling off the Senate floor and into the presence of a radio interviewer, who recorded the Senator as he made his famous statement: "Even if he were mediocre, there are a lot of mediocre judges and people and lawyers. They are entitled to a little representation, aren't they, and a little chance? We can't have all Brandeises and Frankfurters and Cardozos and stuff like that there." To some, that there stuff meant Jews. In any case, the remark was to go down as one of the greatest political blunders in the history of the Senate, and, in the opinion of those most intimately involved in the battle over the nomination, it contributed as much as any other factor to Carswell's defeat. Throughout the country, lawyers and laymen, high and low, arose in indignation at the idea that a man whom his own supporters apparently considered mediocre should be elevated to the Supreme Court, while editorial writers and political cartoonists had a field day unequalled since William H. Vanderbilt said, "The public be damned."

For some time, a rumor had been making the rounds in the capital that Tuttle was not the only one of Carswell's colleagues on the bench to doubt his fitness for a seat on the Supreme Court. Judge John Minor Wisdom, also of the Fifth Circuit Court of Appeals, whose reputation as a jurist matched or even exceeded Tuttle's, was said to have told another judge on that court who proposed circulating a letter of endorsement for Carswell among the court's members, "If you write that letter, I'll write a dissenting opinion." The day after Tuttle's telegrams were put into the record, in another accident of timing Flug happened to run into Caroline Lewis, a reporter for television station WTOP, in Washington, who asked if he had anything new on Carswell. Recalling the latest rumor, he mentioned it to her, and she decided to check it out with Wisdom directly.

When she reached him by telephone, she said she had heard the Attorney General intended to recommend him for the Supreme Court if Carswell lost, whereupon Wisdom laughed and replied that since Mitchell and he didn't see eye to eye, he would never fit into the Administration's Southern strategy. Finally, she pressed him to admit that he had made the remark attributed to him, and he did, saying, "I stand with Tuttle." That evening, Miss Lewis reported the conversation on her news program, and the newspaper reporters, who had been alerted by Flug and Wise, covered the program as a news event.

By this time, Schweiker knew that he could no longer stand by his initial endorsement. Still, he was unwilling to let that be known in too dramatic a fashion—partly because the Administration would resent the effect his switch might have on other Republicans who had also come out for the nominee, but, perhaps more important, because it would encourage Carswell's foes in Pennsylvania to step up their attacks on Scott for continuing to support him. To avoid both of these results, Schweiker arranged with an aide that word of his "reëvaluation" of the nominee be leaked to a couple of reporters in Washington. Then, the same night, while Schweiker was speaking to a high-school group in Philadelphia, newsmen there who had heard the rumor about his change of mind asked him where he stood, and he admitted that he was troubled by the legal and racial aspects of Carswell's record on the bench.

Although the news of Schweiker's move onto the fence travelled from Washington to Philadelphia in a couple of hours, it took five days for the news of his confirmation of the report there to get back to the capital. When it did, Eugene Cowen, a White House liaison man with Congress, hurriedly telephoned Schweiker's office and asked for an appointment that afternoon, a Friday. However, the Senator was in New York, and the date had to be postponed until the following Monday. In the newly subdued White House style, Cowen presented the case for Carswell, and the next day William H. Rehnquist, the Assistant Attorney General for Legal Counsel, who had been responsible for screening Carswell's legal record before he was nominated, visited Schweiker and did his best to rebut the Rosenman letter and the Columbia Law School study. Schweiker heard them out, but by this time it was clear to those who were close to him that he was clambering down the opposite side of the fence he had climbed up on, and his staff began to tell reporters, off the record, that he "seemed to be leaning against the nomination."

Over on the Democratic side of the aisle, a number of senators who had earlier indicated that they meant to vote for Carswell were having second thoughts, too. Senator Burdick, for instance, had voted for the nominee in the Judiciary Committee, but now he let it be known that he was restudying the situation. Burdick was up for reëlection, and North Dakota was a generally conservative state, with a strong Republican Party, few Negroes, and weak labor unions. Burdick knew that he had to have a large share of the Republican votes to win, and he also knew that the voters, and even the newspapers, back home were generally unaware of what had been revealed about Carswell, except for the 1948 speech, and, like many other senators, he considered that no more than an ordinary bit of campaign expediency.

"I wanted to vote for Carswell," Burdick explained later. "In the hearings, he had the endorsement of the Bar Association and purportedly of Tuttle and Wisdom, and for me that was prima-facie evidence that he was qualified, so I voted for him in committee. But then it turned out that he had this huge reversal rate, that Tuttle had retracted his support, and that Wisdom had apparently refused to back him from the start. If those outstanding jurists who knew his work at first hand couldn't go for him, it had to mean that he wasn't qualified after all. That's when the torture set in. I really agonized. There wasn't much external pressure. Oh, lawyers from home wrote me, but I didn't hear from the average fellow. I got some burning from pro-Carswell senators but not much from the other side. All the pressure was from inside myself." The pressure continued to grow, right up to the day of the final vote, and no one, perhaps including Burdick, knew which part of it he would finally succumb to. "Both sides tried to get a promise from me, but I refused," he said.

In the weeks after the Senate hearings ended, the Yale, University of Virginia, and Howard law journals, twenty-one professors from the Stanford University Law School, and the American Federation of Teachers, representing some three hundred and fifty thousand people, issued statements calling on the Senate to reject the nomination. On March 19th, to just about everyone's astonishment, nine of the nineteen faculty members of the Florida State University School of Law, which Carswell had helped found, sent a letter to President Nixon urging him to withdraw the nomination. The chairman of the university's board of regents, D. Burke Kibler III, who was a law partner of Senator Spessard L. Holland, Democrat of Florida, wrote to the school's dean, Joshua Morse, complaining about the faculty members' letter and saying, "I am sure you realize, Josh, how imprudent action such as this makes the task of those of us trying to get adequate funding for the university even more difficult." It was not known whether Kibler's letter alarmed the nine professors, but it didn't seem to have much effect on the rest of the university, for subsequently four hundred and fifty of its students and faculty held a rally to protest the President's choice.

Paradoxically, while opposition to that choice was growing outside the Senate, opposition inside it seemed on the verge of collapsing. Few senators who were engaged in the anti-Carswell side of the debate had much hope that they could prevail, and they were reluctant to put their staffs through the arduous business of writing long speeches and themselves through the risky business of delivering them and arousing the ire of powerful constituents back home—all in a lost cause. Probably the opposition's greatest frustration was its inability to persuade moderate Democrats to share the work load. For instance, Senator Edmund S. Muskie, of Maine, announced his opposition to the nomination very early, but he refused to take an active part in the fight against it.

The lack of this kind of essential support made Bayh's staff increasingly desperate. "We were booking two-hour slots for the senators who were willing to help out—in effect, creating a filibuster, and yet trying not to let it look like a filibuster," Rees said later. "All we were doing was trying to hold the floor. But you need three or four senators at a time to make it work properly, so they can engage in colloquies and at least give the impression that a genuine debate is going on. For example, Senator Bayh had a ten-page speech, and, with colloquies and all, it took him four hours to deliver it. But in general liberals aren't at all good at that sort of thing, because they don't have the practice at it that the Southerners have, and the notion of anything resembling the hated filibuster embarrasses them. Also, we had practically no organization, and most of our men got up and read mail from home and dreary stuff like that. On the eighteenth and nineteenth of March, we had only one man at a time on the floor. It was dammed difficult, and for a time there it looked hopeless. Fortunately, our opponents still thought they had plenty of leeway, and didn't push for a vote. If they had, that would have wrapped it up."

On the nineteenth, it appeared that the affair was to be wrapped up summarily when an article, by Warren Weaver, Jr., appeared in the *Times* stating, in part:

> The campaign to block confirmation of G. Harrold Carswell for the Supreme Court bogged down on the Senate floor today as critics of President Nixon's nominee had trouble sustaining a debate. Confident supporters of Judge Carswell did not even feel required to keep a spokesman in the all-but-empty chamber most of the day as Senator Jacob K. Javits of New York, for the Republicans, and Senator Harold E. Hughes of Iowa, for the Democrats, droned through long readings of critical material. . . . In the light of the day's lack of activity, it appeared doubtful that the Carswell opponents would be able to extend debate beyond next Wednesday or Thursday.

"The Weaver piece was very accurate, but it made us mad as hell," Keefe said afterward. "If senators read it and got the impression that we were just wasting everybody's time, we were through. And, even more important, if it convinced Mansfield that our bad showing meant we couldn't keep our team together, we had no chance. It was already clear that he was beginning to lose interest." Although the Weaver piece nearly destroyed the anti-Carswell cause, in the end the article provided just the spur that was needed. The rest of that day, aides engaged in the fight scoured the Hill looking for some senators who would probably vote against the nomination and who might be persuaded to announce their intentions in advance to give the lagging movement a push.

Within a matter of hours, two unexpected recruits joined up —Vance Hartke, Democrat of Indiana, who was up for reëlection, whose state was conservative, and who was thought to be in some trouble; and Gale W. McGee, Democrat of Wyoming, who had much the same problems. To make it appear that they were merely the first ripples in a rising wave of opposition, Bayh's office called Gravel and told him that the propitious time they had been waiting for had arrived, and he immediately went to the floor to deliver the speech prepared several weeks earlier attacking the nomination. That was expected to have a strong effect on Mansfield, who would see at once that the switch of the only Northern Democrat who had voted for Haynsworth would probably bring about switches by others who had taken the same course.

Then word that Burdick and Schweiker were having second thoughts about their earlier support of Carswell began circulating on the Hill, followed by rumors that four Republicans who had indicated they would vote for Carswell—George D. Aiken and Winston L. Prouty, both of Vermont, along with Marlow Cook, of Kentucky, and Hiram Fong, of Hawaii—were also reconsidering their position, and that Senator J. William Fulbright, Democrat of Arkansas, had almost decided to come out against the nomination. Aiken was the senior member of his party in the Senate and a person of great influence on both sides of the aisle; Fulbright had never backed a civil-rights bill until he supported the Voting Rights Act a few days earlier, and his opposition to Carswell might encourage other Southerners to break loose; and Cook, who had led the fight for Haynsworth, might persuade senators from both the South and the North to join him if he now defected.

Of the four Senators, Cook was the only one who was willing to answer reporters' questions about the rumors. "I could enthusiastically work for and openly endorse the nomination of Clement Haynsworth to the Supreme Court," he told them. "I have not felt that degree of enthusiasm for this nomination." To convince other senators—Mansfield most of all—that the campaign against the nomination was serious, Bayh lined up the dozen or so of his colleagues who had participated in the debate and persuaded them to divide up into teams, each with a captain, and to order their staffs to prepare long and detailed speeches for delivery according to a set schedule.

Tydings took over the largest share of this tedious and inglorious work, and stayed on the floor for hours at a time to make sure that the debate was conducted crisply. He also took the opportunity whenever an uncommitted senator wandered in—usually not to listen but to get away from the daily office grind—to do some quiet lobbying, chiefly among those who were known to be the least susceptible to the standard forms of political pressure. The first member he approached was Senator Fulbright, whose recent break with the South over the Voting Rights Act seemed an encouraging sign. Tydings had been a U.S. Attorney before coming to the Senate, and his courtroom experience had made him a tough and forcefull debater, but in this case he dispensed with that kind of approach and relied instead on gentle persuasion. After pointing out the graver flaws in Carswell's record, he reminded Fulbright of the vital role the Supreme Court played in a critically divided society and of the responsibility that each senator had under these circumstances to cast his vote as conscience, not politics, dictated. Fulbright listened attentively, and afterward he conceded that Tydings' arguments had impressed him.

Brooke had asked everyone on his side not to approach Senator Margaret Chase Smith, the redoubtable lady from Maine, because she resented any intrusion when she was faced with a decision of this magnitude. But Tydings decided to take the risk. Sitting down with her one day, he began talking about the time, a few years back, when Edward Kennedy had sponsored the nomination of a Boston politician named Francis X. Morrisey to the federal bench. At the time, Tydings told her, he had been scheduled to go abroad with Kennedy shortly after the Senate voted on Morrisey. But then the nominee began, as Tydings put it, "to smell a little," and he decided that perhaps it would be wise to leave on the trip early, to avoid the dilemma of either voting for Morrisey and betraying his own conscience or voting against him and betraying his friendship with Kennedy. Finally, though, Tydings attended the hearings on the nomination, and decided that Morrisey wasn't fit to be on any bench. "I saw that I couldn't dodge it then, so I told Ted I would have to vote against him," Tydings said to Mrs. Smith. "In my opinion, Carswell is worse than Morrisey, and none of us can avoid facing our responsibility." Mrs. Smith seemed moved by the story, but, as always, she remained noncommital.

A few days later, Carswell's backers also used the Morrisey case to defend their side. At one point in the debate, Senators Gurney and Dole engaged in a colloquy designed to remind their colleagues that while Senator Kennedy was a leading opponent of the present nominee because of his alleged lack of credentials, the Senator had been the leading proponent of the Morrisey nomination despite that candidate's proved lack of credentials. Kennedy was in the cloakroom, and when he was told what had been said he hurried out to the floor and joined the debate. As it happened, he had intended to bring up the Morrisey episode himself, and now he took advantage of the opening provided by Gurney and Dole and told them that when a large number of senators opposed that nomination he had withdrawn it, on the ground that it was bad policy to put a man on the bench if so many senators were against him. Now, with a broad smile, Kennedy suggested that the opposing side might follow the same course. Morrisey was not brought up again.

Ordinarily, speeches on the floor of the Senate during such debates have little effect, since few members attend these rhetorical exercises, and those who do rarely listen. However, one speech that was made during this debate had a marked effect, not on one of the participants but on the presiding officer—who is usually a freshman senator unless the Vice-President himself is in the chair. Late on a Friday afternoon, a week and a half before the final vote was taken, Senator Goodell, who had been waiting for over an hour to fill his slot in Bayh's schedule, finally got the floor. "By then, I realized that just about everything I had planned to say had already been said," he recalled afterward. "Since Mansfield had announced that we would adjourn when I finished, there was no need for me to make the speech just to hold the floor, which was the main reason I was there, of course. So I decided to mention of couple of things I hadn't heard said and insert the rest of my speech in the record. I was just about to do that when I looked up and saw that Marlow Cook was presiding. So I made a four-minute speech aimed at him. My main point was that Carswell could still be on the Supreme Court in the year 2000. When I said that, Marlow jumped straight up in the air."

The unexpected response from the nation's leading lawyers to the Rosenman group's appeal led Bayh to conclude that support from the legal community at large might be the final influence needed to bring uncommitted senators into his camp. As a further step in this direction, he decided that it would be helpful if some of the top lawyers in Washington's most prominent law firms who had formerly served in high posts in the government were to put their prestige and their contacts to work in a more direct fashion than Rosenman and his three associates had. To this end, Bayh got in touch with a number of men who possessed such credentials—among them Joseph A. Califano, Jr., President Johnson's top aide; Harry McPherson, another Johnson aide; Lee White, special counsel to Presidents Kennedy and Johnson; Lloyd Cutler, director of the President's Commission on the Causes and Prevention of Violence; Clifford Alexander, former member of the Equal Employment Opportunity Commission; and John Douglas and Stephen Pollak, former Assistant Attorneys General. The men, all of whom were eager to do whatever they could to defeat the nomination, gathered in Bayh's office on March 19th.

"We went over head-count sheets and discussed ways of

influencing individual senators through their more important constituents and campaign contributors," Califano recounted later. "Bayh was in his shirtsleeves, and it reminded me of going over head counts with L.B.J."

The group devised and agreed upon a number of tactics —a high-level attack on the American Bar Association's Committee on the Federal Judiciary for its careless examination of Carswell's qualifications and for its decision to make, in his case, only a distinction between the terms "qualified" and "not qualified" instead of employing the more precisely descriptive terms that had been used in evaluating Supreme Court nominees in the past; refutation of Attorney General Mitchell's public claim that the American Bar Association had "unanimously" found the nominee "highly recommended," whereas actually only twelve of the hundred and fifty thousand lawyers who belonged to the Association had made the determination, and then had said only that he was "qualified;" and a concerted effort to get in touch with lawyers throughout the country who might be able to influence members of the Senate. To a large extent, this last approach had to be kept secret, in order to protect those who were unwilling to let their part in the anti-Carswell campaign be known. To keep the operation more or less under cover, Bayh set up a separate office in his suite and assigned a volunteer named Ronald Platt, who had taken a week off from his job with the Matt Reese political consulting firm, to coördinate all the contacts made. Only Platt was to know who was calling whom and what the results were.

When the meeting broke up, Califano and Cutler went directly to Califano's office at Arnold & Porter and drafted a telegram to Walsh, the head of the American Bar Association's committee, stating that Carswell failed to meet "the minimum requirements of professional ability and judicial temperament to sit on the Supreme Court" and requesting that the committee reconvene to hear the most recent objections to the nomination and then present the facts to the Senate. Once the text was ready, the two men got on separate telephones and talked eight leading members of the bar into signing it—the deans of the Harvard, Yale, University of Pennsylvania, and U.C.L.A. Law Schools; Rosenman and Plimpton, two of the four authors of the open letter; Neal Rutledge, a prominent Miami lawyer and the son of a former associate justice; and Warren Christopher, Deputy Attorney General under President Johnson.

"It was a hell of a tough document, and we had some doubt about whether the men we called would sign it," Califano said afterward. "I was especially uneasy about Mr. Plimpton, but he merely suggested a couple of minor changes and agreed on the spot. I understand that he was an absolute tiger throughout this whole thing."

Califano and Cutler decided not to make the telegram public, because they feared that its disclosure would be interpreted by Walsh as an attempt to force his hand. As it happened, Walsh didn't answer the wire until the case was closed, and, as far as was known, he didn't mention it to the other members of the committee. After a week had passed without a reply, Cutler and Califano drafted another telegram, signed by the same men, and demanded a response. Once again Walsh ignored their request, whereupon they released the text of both wires to the press. That, too, had no effect on Walsh, but it had a strong effect on Horsky, who was said to be infuriated by Walsh's high-handed behavior and edged closer to making the move that several people had been pushing him toward—disclosure of his meeting with Carswell the night before the Senate hearings on the nomination began. Although Horsky held off for a time, his private discussions about the episode soon leaked out, and before many days had passed just about everyone on the Hill had heard about it.

During this period, John Douglas, one of the other participants at the lawyers' meeting in Bayh's office, set out to pull off a scheme of his own—a letter against the nomination to be signed by former clerks to Supreme Court justices. Within a matter of days, more than two hundred of them had signed the letter—a list ranging alphabetically from Dean Acheson, former Secretary of State, to Edwin Zimmerman, former Assistant Attorney General. On the theory that a large proportion of the law professors in the country had studied at Harvard and Yale Law Schools, Douglas then asked Deans Bok and Pollak to get in touch with whomever they or anyone else in their schools knew on law faculties everywhere.

Again within a matter of days, letters opposing the nomination poured in from the faculties of most of the major and many of the minor law schools in the country. Heads of local bar associations rallied to the cause, too, and then specialists in various legal fields added their protests—among them that in property law Carswell had been unable "to state the facts in any comprehensible fashion," that in tax law he had "adduced conclusions . . . unsupported by any reasoning," that in criminal law his opinions were "characterized, at best, by unimaginative, mechanical mediocrity," and that in contract law he had shown that he was "an absurd constructionist."

In most cases, the undecided senators who were the principal targets of the lawyers' work were captured without being aware of the elaborate, and largely indirect, efforts made to line them up. For instance, in the course of an attempt to get Senator Frank E. Moss, Democrat of Utah, to join the opposition, Dean Pollak recalled that a former dean of the University of Pennsylvania Law School was close to several professors at the University of Utah Law School, so Pollak called him and he called his friends, who immediately began organizing the faculty there and working on prominent lawyers and businessmen in Salt Lake City. Shortly afterward, Senator Moss announced that he would vote against Carswell. When the rumor that Senator Fulbright was unhappy about the nomination reached P. J. Mode, he called Dean Bok and asked if he knew anyone who was close to Fulbright. Bok replied that he didn't but that Plimpton was close to George Ball, former Under-Secretary of State, who was close to Fulbright. Bok asked Plimpton to get in touch with Ball, and when Ball learned that his old friend the chairman of the Foreign Relations Committee was badly in need of advice on this domestic matter he dropped in to see him.

The lawyers working with Bayh were astonished by the response to their appeals. "It was fantastic," Califano said not long ago. "Those of us who knew government from the inside tried to recall all the important contacts we had, however remote, and we used them to the hilt. Ordinarily, most people in this town are reluctant to use up their credit with somebody unless some personal advantage is involved. But this time nobody cared about anything like that. One of the lawyers I called was a man of considerable influence in his state, and I hardly knew him and had nothing to offer in return. He responded immediately, and said that he was utterly opposed to Carswell and that he was willing to do anything—anything at all—to stop him from going on the Court. Time after time, men said things like 'I wanted to help, but I didn't know anything could be done. Just tell me what to do and I'll do it.'

"I discovered a widespread apprehension among lawyers that the integrity of the judiciary was at stake. A tremendous number of lawyers around the country are deeply disturbed by what's been happening to the law *within* the government and about how it's being perverted for political ends. I talked to men who have done nothing but practice straight law and who were frantic about what's been going on at the Justice Department, about its part in carrying out the Southern strategy and turning out all those phony and un-Constitutional anti-crime bills. A lot of new law-school graduates from the top schools won't go near the place now, whereas they used to flock there to get experience. And men who've been in the Department for ten or twenty years are leaving in droves. Anyway, the lawyers of America were really shaken by the Carswell nomination. They set out to defeat it, and they succeeded."

On March 22nd, three days after the group of lawyers went to work, Senator Fred R. Harris, Democrat of Oklahoma, proposed on a television interview show in the capital that the best way to settle the Senate debate on whether Carswell's nomination should be confirmed might be to recommit the nomination to the Judiciary Committee for further study. This parliamentary device was by no means unusual, but it had not been suggested before in the Carswell case, and it struck everyone as perhaps an ideal way out of what was becoming an embarrassingly awkward dilemma for many members of the Senate.

By that time, the feeling there was that if senators were free to vote as they wished, Carswell would be overwhelmingly defeated; in fact, one conservative Southerner who publicly supported him confessed in private that if the nomination were to be decided by secret ballot he would get perhaps ten votes. Recommitting the nomination, most agreed, would let those who wanted to oppose it, but didn't dare to for political reasons, say that they merely wanted answers to the questions which had been raised since the hearings ended before they sent Judge Carswell to the Supreme Court—an explanation that neither the President nor ordinary citizens could decently argue with. At the same time, it was generally admitted that if the nomination was sent back to committee it would die there, because its opponents on the committee would block action on it until either the President or Carswell himself withdrew it to avoid further humiliation.

Senator Fulbright particularly favored this solution—in fact, he had recommended it to Harris—and the day after it was broached on television he told Bayh that he not only would vote for a motion to recommit the nomination but would offer the motion personally if Bayh liked. Bayh mentioned this to Majority Leader Mansfield, who instructed an aide to poll the Democrats on how they would vote on such a proposal. On March 23rd, two days before the Easter recess, Mansfield told Bayh and Brooke that a recommittal motion would probably carry if they could produce twelve Republican votes in favor of it. Brooke had been working ceaselessly among his fellow-Republicans, and by this time he was fairly confident that six of them—Schweiker, Mathias, Packwood, Hatfield, Percy, and Prouty—would line up with those who had already announced their opposition to Carswell—Goodell, Javits, Case, and Brooke himself—to make ten votes. If Cook came around, as Brooke believed he would, that would provide the eleventh vote and it would almost certainly persuade two or three other Republicans to go along with him.

That day, a conference committee between the Senate and the House approved the Elementary and Secondary Education Act and sent it to both bodies for a final vote. To the dismay of Southerners in the Senate, the conferees had nullified the bill's so-called Stennis amendment, which had been tacked on as a rider by Senator John Stennis, Democrat of Mississippi, to require that the civil-rights guidelines, which were applied to

seven states in the Deep South, be applied uniformly throughout the country. The purpose of the amendment was to compel
the Justice Department to deploy its already undermanned
forces outside the South and thereby weaken their effect where
it was most needed. When the conference report reached the
Senate, Mansfield—now clearly impressed by the Bayh-Brooke
teamwork and the growing roster of Carswell's opponents—
announced that the report would be the pending order of
business.

The Southerners saw that Mansfield had outmaneuvered
them once again, and intended to use the report, as he had
used the Voting Rights Act earlier, to force them to accept
a bill they didn't want so they could get to vote on Carswell
before the opposition built up any more strength. Minority
Whip Griffin immediately came to their defense and angrily
objected to the move, but Mansfield, unruffled as always,
replied that, under the rules of the Senate, conference reports
took precedence over bills and executive nominations.

By now, it was clear to anyone who could count that the
nomination was in grave peril—anyone, that is, outside the
White House, where confidence in Carswell's confirmation was
still high. One prominent Republican senator was later to
suggest that the White House staff be required to take a re-
fresher course in addition, but others put the failure down to
the intelligence system there, for although Schweiker, Mathias,
Packwood, Percy, and Fulbright had been shaken loose from
the pro-Carswell column, no one on the liaison staff downtown seemed to be aware of it. Around this time, Brooke happened to be at the White House on other business, and he
took the opportunity to tell the President, "I want you to
know that I am working day and night to defeat your nomination to the Supreme Court." Mr. Nixon, who apparently con-

cluded that Brooke was merely playing to the liberal and black grandstands back home, smiled indulgently and went on with the previous conversation. On the afternoon of March 24th, Senator Griffin visited the White House and assured John Ehrlichman, one of the President's two or three closest advisers, that the nomination was in grave danger. Ehrlichman refused to believe it.

"We sort of got to rely on the staff down there," Bayh remarked later. "Its failure to assess the situation clearly meant that the enormous pressure the White House can always exert wasn't present until it was too late."

Finally, Griffin's warning was checked out, and when the President was told of the danger he summoned Deputy Attorney General Kleindienst, who was acting head of the Department of Justice while Attorney General Mitchell was on vacation in Florida, and angrily told him that since he was officially responsible for screening candidates for federal judgeships and for getting him into the Carswell mess, he had better get them all out of it.

On March 25th, Bayh met in the Majority Leader's office with the other leaders of the anti-Carswell forces to discuss what might be done to obtain two more weeks before the vote was taken, a period that all of them agreed was essential to create the maximum opposition at the proper time. Bayh asked how the others felt about filibustering to delay a vote that long, and Javits flatly refused to engage in one, saying, "I will not filibuster against my own President." Hart refused, too, because he opposed filibusters in principle, and Tydings and Brooke took no position. Although Bayh felt that they weren't doing their utmost if they didn't use whatever means were available to them, he dropped the idea of a filibuster.

With that much settled, they turned to a discussion of a

maneuver that Mansfield had tested on Carswell's supporters
earlier that day on the floor—an agreement by which they
would allow a vote on the education bill on April 1st if
Bayh's side would agree to a vote on recommittal on April
6th and, that failing, to a vote on confirmation on April 8th.
Hruska feared that the opposition might filibuster if he refused
to accept this arrangement, so he had agreed to it; now, once
the filibuster idea was discarded, the Bayh-Brooke side agreed,
too.

While that provided the two weeks, it also raised the question of who would be the best person to move for recommittal.
Bayh mentioned Fulbright's offer, but Brooke was against ac-
cepting it, and pointed out that the White House was still unaware of Fulbright's change of mind, and that if it saw him
break ranks and join the leadership of the opposition more
danger signals would be raised all over the place and pressure
would be turned on at once. Instead, Brooke went on, it would
be far better for Bayh himself to make the motion. "As surprising as it may seem, you should do it because they don't dislike
you downtown," he explained. "They feel you're simply doing
what a liberal senator should do."

Late the same afternoon, Bayh offered the motion that both
sides had accepted—in the form of a unanimous-consent agreement—and it was adopted at once. Then Fulbright took the
floor and announced that he would vote for recommittal, although he said nothing about how he stood on confirmation.
Hatfield also announced that he would vote for recommittal
and went on to indicate that he would vote against confirmation as well by releasing the text of a telegram he had sent to
the President urging him to withdraw the nomination as the
only way to resolve "the crisis of confidence that confronts our
governmental process."

In a radio interview that day, Packwood angrily attacked the recommittal move, saying, "There are probably six to eight senators who don't want [Carswell] and who don't have the guts to vote against him." Then he demonstrated that he wasn't one of them by announcing that he would oppose both recommittal and confirmation. It was widely assumed that the White House had put Packwood up to this, but he privately denied it and said that actually he was sorry he had made such an intemperate remark about his colleagues, even though he felt it was true. Still, one anti-Carswell aide said that at the time "the soundings coming out of Packwood's office turned bad, so bad that his name was placed on the questionable list." To put it back firmly where Packwood said it would be, appeals were made to some leading members of the Dorchester Conference, a group of several hundred liberal Republicans that Packwood had organized in Oregon some years earlier for a dual purpose—to air topics that were not often aired in orthodox Republican circles, and to help him reach the Senate—and they went to work to make sure that he kept his promise to vote against Carswell.

Despite the growing list of defectors, the White House didn't seem unduly alarmed and did nothing more than put out a statement saying, "The President is firm in his support for Judge Carswell."

On the day that the unanimous-consent agreement was reached, the Washington *Post* ran a front-page story describing the meeting that took place in Carswell's Washington hotel, on January 26th, at which Horsky and Ramsey met with Carswell to ask, on behalf of the American Bar Association's Committee on the Federal Judiciary, what his role had been in transforming the segregated municipal golf club in Tallahassee into a segregated private club in 1956 to circumvent the Supreme Court ruling prohibiting segregated public recreation facilities. Then the article went on to assert that Carswell had admitted to the two men that while he was serving as U.S. Attorney he had been "an incorporator of a segregated Tallahassee country club on the night before he swore to the Senate that he had no such role." (Actually, the story had been broken several days earlier by Fred P. Graham, of the New York *Times*, but the editors had buried it in the back pages in the first edition and then, deciding that it was "too soft," had cut it out entirely.)

Now that the story was no longer mere gossip, Flug telephoned Horsky and asked what conditions he wanted before he would recount the details of his meeting with Carswell in a letter or a memorandum. After thinking it over, Horsky replied that if a member of the Judiciary Committee asked him for such a document he would honor the request but that under no circumstances would he divulge the A.B.A. committee's deliberations on the subject. Flug informed Kennedy, Bayh, Tydings, and Hart of the offer, and got authorization from Kennedy to make the request officially. Flug passed on Kennedy's request, and Tydings also called Horsky to accept his offer personally. Following several lengthy telephone conversations with Flug, who acted as intermediary, Horsky drafted a memorandum describing the encounter, got Ramsey to approve it, and sent copies to Kennedy and Tydings.

The memorandum, which came to be known as the Horsky memo, began by stating that Horsky and Ramsey had visited Carswell at the committee chairman's request to ask about the golf-club episode. After that, the key section stated, "Mr. Horsky, who had brought to the meeting photostatic copies of a number of papers having to do with the corporate organization of the club, then showed Judge Carswell the papers from the Certificate of Incorporation on which the names and signatures of the incorporators of the club appeared, showing him as an incorporator."

Since Carswell had assured the committee, under oath and on two separate days, that he was utterly unfamiliar with the contents of these papers, there could be no doubt now that he had deceived the Senate. As it was, though, Horsky's revelation came too late to have much effect. By this time, most of the senators who were finally to vote for Carswell had already announced their intention, and they were, as the Washington saying goes, "locked in." For instance, a couple of days before news of the Horsky memo was published, Senator John Sherman Cooper, Republican of Kentucky and one of the most respected men in the Senate, had announced that he would vote for Carswell and then refused to withdraw his support despite the appearance of the memo and the pleas of some of his oldest friends and closest associates that he change his mind.

Cooper had provided a good part of the ten-vote margin against Haynsworth's nomination, for when he revealed that he would oppose it there had been a stampede of other Republicans to line up with him. Cooper's endorsement of Carswell shocked liberals and moderates both in the Senate and out, since he had often been their leader—in the fight against the A.B.M., for example—and was almost always their ally. Perhaps the most surprised of them all was Clarence Mitchell, who had talked with Cooper before both the Haynsworth and the Carswell votes and had come away as strongly convinced by his second visit as he had been by the first that the Senator would vote no.

To Cooper, the cases were essentially different. "My general position has been to support a President's decision in such matters," he explained later. "I expected to support Abe Fortas for Chief Justice, but then the facts that were brought out changed my mind. In the Haynsworth affair, I felt that although he hadn't personally profited from his decisions in the cases where he held stock in companies that were litigants before his court, he had violated the federal statute and the judicial canons, both of which instruct judges to disqualify themselves in such cases. Since Haynsworth was a good lawyer, he must have known this, and yet he neither disqualified himself nor disclosed his violations during the Senate hearings on his nomination. That forced me to oppose him. With Carswell, the main questions for me were whether he was a racist and whether he had deceived the committee about the golf-club incident. To vote against him on the ground of the 1948 speech, where he promised he would always defend white supremacy, I would have had to conclude that his bias had continued. I read most of the hearing record and twenty of his opinions, and I couldn't conclude that. While he wasn't as competent a judge as could have been nominated, I finally decided that to vote against him I would have had to be as biassed as they said *he* was. On the second question, I would have had to be convinced that the golf club was made into a private corporation solely to exclude Negroes. That wasn't it at all. The place was bankrupt, and they were trying to keep it open."

Passing over affidavits from numerous Tallahassee citizens, black and white and high and low, along with newspaper ariticles published at the time stating that the exclusion of Negroes was generally accepted as the reason for making the public course private, and also passing over the question of how a municipal facility—whether it is a waterworks or a golf club—can go bankrupt, Senator Cooper went on to say that neither had he found the Judge dishonest in his appearance before the Judiciary Committee. "In the first morning's hearing, Carswell admitted two or three times after his first lie that he had been an incorporator," the Senator explained. "Since he admitted this, however belatedly, I couldn't see how he had deceived the committee."

Ignoring Carswell's repeated insistence on the day *after* these admissions that he had never seen the papers in question and had no idea of what they contained, Senator Cooper went on to concede that Carswell did not have an exemplary judicial record. Just the same, he added, he did not feel that the Judge had been unfair in civil-rights cases, and cited the decision in which Carswell ordered his own barber to serve black customers, an order desegregating rest rooms in Talla-

hassee, a ruling that a one-hour notice before holding demon-
strations was too arbitrary, and his role in setting up the
Florida State University Law School and insisting that it be
open to all races. To Carswell's opponents, of course, these
cases seemed like a machine-gunner's putting a couple of
blanks among the live bullets in his ammunition belt. As for
stories about Carswell's hostility to civil-rights lawyers, Senator
Cooper argued that most of the testimony on this point was
hearsay, although he failed to explain how the three witnesses
who testified about it had relied on hearsay when they had
discussed only their own experiences in Judge Carswell's court.

In the end, the sole argument against Carswell that the
Senator found persuasive was one made by Senator Hart—
namely, that whether or not Carswell was a racist, the black
community believed that he was, which was just as bad. "That
point had some weight with me," Cooper went on. "But then
I wondered if I could decide the issue on that basis when I
believed he had no animus toward Negroes. On that basis, one
would have to oppose *any* judge from the South, because every
judge, as Justice Holmes once said, is to an extent a product of
his environment, like anyone else." Environment notwithstand-
ing, no one had ever levelled the charge of racism against such
Judges as Tuttle and Wisdom, not to mention a number of
other Southern jurists.

Finally, Senator Cooper disagreed that Carswell's record
on the bench was an obstacle. "That argument against him
rested upon subjective judgments concerning his ability and
capacity for growth, which are a matter of speculative opinion," he explained. To Carswell's critics, there was little of a
speculative nature about his record on habeas-corpus cases or
on his having been unanimously reversed in seventeen civil-
and human-rights cases. As for subjective judgments, few sena-

tors who felt free to decide the issue on its merits were willing, in these perilous times, to put a man with such a record on the Supreme Court, where he might sit for thirty years or more, in the hope that he would turn out all right.

No one in Washington questioned Senator Cooper's sincerity, which was regarded with much the same awe as his rocklike integrity. In some quarters, it was speculated that his staff, which was largely conservative, had been dismayed by his leadership of the fight against the A.B.M. and his pivotal role in blocking Haynsworth and may not have fully informed him about Carswell's record. Various other explanations went the rounds, among them one to the effect that President Nixon had promised to make him the Administration's leader in the Senate debate on the Strategic Arms Limitation Treaty (SALT) talks in exchange for his vote for Carswell. But others felt that no one, including the President, would dare offer a man like Cooper a deal of any kind.

On this point, the Senator himself said later, "The President didn't talk to me about Carswell on his own initiative. I just happened to be in the White House during the SALT discussions, and I told him that I had decided to vote for Carswell. In fact, I had made up my mind to a week before. Having told him this, I said that I would make a statement and a speech about my position when the Senate reconvened after Easter. Afterward, one of the President's aides called me and asked if I would announce my decision right away—four days earlier than I had planned. Since I was going to announce it anyway, I agreed."

Still, there were lingering doubts, because he was not content merely to cast his vote in favor of the nomination but worked actively for Carswell among other senators. As one of them said later, "John was really out there in the trenches on this one."

Soon after Cooper's announcement, the two other leading Republicans in the Senate—George Aiken, of Vermont, and John J. Williams, of Delaware—also came out for Carswell. The earlier rumor that Aiken was about to join the opposition had ignored the fact that he had voted against a major Presidential nomination only once in his thirty years in the Senate, and now he jovially told a colleague that he would vote for any-one the President named, unless the fellow had murdered someone—lately. As for Williams, who has been called the conscience of the Senate, one of his fellow-Republicans said after his public statement, "It's true that he has a big con-science, but it's also true that he usually brings it down on the side of conservative causes."

Around this time, the White House released a telegram from eleven of Carswell's eighteen active and semi-retired colleagues on the Fifth Circuit Court of Appeals endorsing him. This move, which was interpreted as an attempt to cancel the effect of the Horsky memo, was credited to Klein-dienst. It was also put down as an exceedingly clumsy maneu-ver, because it demonstrated not so much that nearly two-thirds of Carswell's fellow-judges supported him as it pointed out that more than a third of them opposed him. "Haynsworth didn't solicit his fellow-judges for an endorsement, as Carswell did," Senator Cook said later. "They made it on their own initiative. Carswell had to solicit, and even then he couldn't get seven out of the eighteen. There were judges who said they absolutely wouldn't endorse him. Imagine what they faced. If Carswell went on the Supreme Court, their decisions would be subject to his review and comments. Or if he lost they would have to face him constantly in person. That they still refused to endorse him had a big effect on many senators."

Some of them were also said to have been affected by a state-ment that Judge Wisdom made explaining why he had refused to put his name on the telegram. "I think the Court [of Appeals] has no business as a court endorsing or not endorsing a man as a nominee for the Supreme Court," he said. "It seems to me it violates separation of powers. But when it comes to individual opinion, I think that this moment is not the time to appoint a reactionary to the Supreme Court. It shows a lack of understanding of the urgency of the situation."

During the Easter recess, most senators went home to get a bit of rest and to mend a few fences. Many of them ran into surprisingly deep feeling against the President's choice for the Supreme Court, but few of them found quite the angry mood that confronted Senator Fong, of Hawaii, when he got home. Although he had good reason to oppose Carswell—chiefly because of the islanders' resentment of any taint of racism—Fong had voted for the nominee in the Judiciary Committee and was expected to support him the rest of the way. At the beginning of his visit, the Senator announced that while he would vote against recommital, he hadn't yet decided whether or not he would vote for confirmation.

Subsequently, Fong's chief aide, Robert Carson, was asked what pressures had been brought to bear for and against Carswell in the Senator's case, and he answered, "There was no pressure on the Senator. No one would try to exert pressure on him because it is well known that he is not susceptible to any form of pressure. On an issue like this, he simply takes a judicious stance. He gathers all the facts, put them in the proper legal and social balance, and then, keeping an entirely open mind, decides the issue solely on its merits."

It was a nice civics-book description of a senator at work, but it was somewhat at odds with the facts. Actually, Fong was probably the object of as much pressure as any other Republican senator, and just about everyone involved believed that of the Republicans who finally voted against Carswell he was among the few who had decided the issue entirely on the political merits. To begin with, the White House had promised him a federal judgeship for one of his friends and help in setting up an East-West trade center in Hawaii if he voted for Haynsworth. He did, but when that nomination went down to defeat the White House offered the same rewards for his vote in favor of Carswell. That, it was reported, didn't sit well with Fong, and to help him take a judicious stance the other side began to create counterpressure.

This assignment fell to Gary Burns Sellers, a young lawyer who served as one of the top commanders of Nader's Raiders and was that outfit's specialist on Capitol Hill. At the time, Sellers was on loan to Representative Philip Burton, Democrat of California, to help in his efforts to devise a coal-mine-safety bill, and Burton gave him time, if he saw fit, to work against the nomination. At the outset, Sellers had concentrated on stirring up opposition to Carswell in Hawaii during his spare time. (Most of the work had to be done by telephone, and Fong was an ideal subject for Sellers to work on in his spare time, since the difference between Washington time and Hawaii time allowed him to spend his evenings in Washington talking to people during their afternoons in Hawaii.)

At first, Sellers was at a loss about what was the best way to proceed, but then he recalled a classmate and fraternity brother from his days at the University of Michigan Law School named Stuart Ho, whose father was reputed to own a sizable part of Honolulu and was undoubtedly a man of great influence. Sellers rang up Honolulu Information and learned not only that young Ho had three telephone numbers, indicating that he was perhaps a man of some influence, too, but that one of them was the number of the state legislature. Sellers called this number and found that Ho, a Democrat, was the majority leader of the house of representatives.

Sellers got through to Ho after several calls, reminded him of their university ties, and went on to describe what was happening in Washington over the Carswell nomination. To Sellers' delight, it turned out that Ho had introduced a resolution condemning the nomination and had just been wondering how he could pry it out of the committee where it was languishing. Sellers told him that Fong was one of the swing votes, and urged Ho to press for action on his resolution as one way of bringing pressure to bear on Fong. Ho promised to do what he could, and then gave Sellers the names of several people in Washington who were close to Fong and might be able to influence him.

Sellers got in touch with them at once, and while they went about softening up the Senator he tracked down, through another contact from his university days, a couple of newspapermen in Hawaii. When he got through to them on the telephone, he found that, like Ho, they were unaware of Fong's pivotal role in the fight against Carswell. Assuring Sellers that they were dead set against the nomination, they promised to help and asked what they could do. He said that the most effective approach would probably be to hammer away at how crucial Fong's part in the affair was, since this would encourage his constituents to write and urge him to oppose the nominee. "That was what we needed most," Sellers said afterward. "We wanted Fong to come into his office when he got back to Washington and find letters stacked to the ceiling."

143

To keep the pile of mail and the pressure on Fong mounting, Sellers called his press contacts in Honolulu almost every day to fill them in on the latest developments—usually the news that another senator had come out against Carswell, which, Sellers pointed out, made Fong's role even more crucial. The papers played up these stories and ran editorials demanding that Fong stand up against the nomination, whatever the President's displeasure. One dividend of the campaign was that it gave Ho the lever to pry his resolution out of the lower house and push it through both bodies. At the same time, Representative Patsy Mink, Democrat of Hawaii, who was also home for the holiday, went around the islands attacking Carswell and calling on the voters to demand that Fong vote against him. If he didn't, she told several audiences, she might be compelled to run against Fong when he came up for reëlection the following fall.

In the end, these efforts created a typhoon of feeling against Carswell. When Fong was asked by reporters, just before he left for Washington, where he now stood, he replied that he still opposed recommittal but that he had examined the merits of the issue and had decided he would have to vote against confirmation, too.

Sellers' attempts to persuade other senators to consider the same merits that had brought Fong around proved less successful. The next target was Senator James B. Pearson, Republican of Kansas, whose political views ranged from moderate to liberal but whose state was inflexibly conservative. Pearson was Brooke's closest friend in the Senate, but Brooke had not approached him for his vote, because he knew that leaders of the Republican Party in Kansas had threatened Pearson with the fiercest primary fight of his career in 1972 if he opposed the President now. Once again Sellers turned to his university friends and acquaintances, and finally located several alumni who were lawyers in Kansas. He explained the deep concern in Washington over the prospect of Carswell's reaching the Supreme Court, and, as before, just about everybody offered to help. They gathered signatures on petitions, arranged for letter-writing campaigns, and appealed directly to Pearson's closest friends.

While Pearson listened patiently to all these appeals and agreed that the arguments had some merits, he held to his intention to support the President. Then recalling that the Senator was known as a deeply religious man, Sellers discussed this with a friend in Washington who came from Kansas and who knew Pearson's minister there. The friend was as concerned about the nomination as Sellers, and agreed to telephone the minister and ask him to help. When the request was made, the minister replied that he had already tried and had failed.

Undaunted, Sellers set out to verify a rumor that had been going around for some time—that Judge Carswell had told the chancellor of the University of Kansas, who was a native of Florida and a friend, that he must have moved North "to get away from the niggers," a move that, according to the rumor, Carswell said he had been contemplating, too. The chancellor was on vacation in Mexico, but Sellers tracked him down and called to ask that he publicly confirm the story if it was true. The chancellor refused to make any comment. He also refused to confirm the rumor privately, which might have been enough to persuade Pearson to change his vote. Unaware of Sellers' appeals, Kennedy's aide Flug made a similar call, with similar results. "I knew that if we got the chancellor to tell the story, that alone would knock Carswell out," he said later. "I pleaded with the man for confirmation, but I just got nowhere."

Still undaunted, Sellers called a couple of faculty members at the University of Kansas School of Medicine and described his efforts to verify the rumor. When the chancellor alighted from the airplane bringing him home from vacation, practically the entire medical faculty was waiting on the tarmac, and their spokesman demanded that they be told whether the story was true. Again the chancellor refused to answer, saying only that he might not get the usual state grants if he rocked the boat. While that may have seemed to be an admission that Carswell had made the reported remark, it wasn't enough for Pearson, and he stayed with the Administration.

Sellers also went after Senator Jennings W. Randolph, Democrat of West Virginia, in the hope that if a senator from a border state were shaken loose senators from the Deep South who were unhappy about the nomination might use the opening as an escape route. Randolph was due to come up for reelection in 1972, and it was believed that his opponent in the Democratic primary would be Representative Ken Hechler, author of "The Bridge at Remagen," who had settled in Huntington some years earlier to launch a political career. Since West Virginia is a desperately poor state, with what seems to be an incurable unemployment problem, its voters had more to worry about than whether a "son of the South" was being mistreated by Northerners, and this inclined Sellers to believe that Randolph would be taking little or no political risk if he opposed Carswell but would get some valuable credit with liberals at home who might otherwise line up behind Hechler.

To get this message across, Sellers and a couple of associates got in touch with the lobby that, under Hechler's leadership, had pushed through compensation for West Virginia coal miners who had contracted black-lung disease. While this group worked on Randolph, Sellers worked on his staff, who promised to do what they could. Then he turned to John D. Rockefeller IV, a Democrat and the West Virginia secretary of state, and asked *his* aides to do what they could to persuade him to persuade his Republican father-in-law, Senator Percy, to persuade Randolph to join the opposition. Randolph wouldn't be persuaded. "In fact, he wouldn't even swerve," one of the men involved in this effort said later. "He's completely out of touch with the times, and just lumbers on like an aged elephant headed for its doom."

His doom promised to be fairly comfortable. Just before the

147

Haynsworth vote, the Administration announced, through Randolph's office and without mentioning Hechler, a three-million-dollar grant for an urban-renewal project in Hechler's district. Randolph, as it turned out, voted for Haynsworth.

U p to the Easter recess, Carswell's critics made no serious mistakes, but during the recess one of them, a newcomer to the fray, made such a spectacular blunder that he endangered the entire cause. Near the end of March, Senator Alan Cranston, a liberal Democrat from California, heard that Charles F. Wilson, a Negro who had written the Judiciary Committee stating that in his numerous appearances as a private civil-rights lawyer before Judge Carswell he had been treated with unfailing courtesy, had later told Vincent H. Cohen, another Negro lawyer, that the letter was a fraud; Wilson had signed it, Cohen told Cranston, but he hadn't written it. According to the story, the author of the letter was Assistant Attorney General Rehnquist, who had taken this step on Kleindienst's orders, after it was learned that Wilson now worked for the government—for the Equal Employment Opportunity Commission in Washington. According to Cohen, he had asked Wilson to sign an affidavit relating this episode, but Wilson had declined, whereupon Cohen drew up his own affidavit describing the conversation.

The issue was of some importance, for the Wilson letter constituted the only favorable report on Judge Carswell's treat-

ment of civil-rights lawyers. Ten others had testified or submitted affidavits stating that he had been unfailingly rude to
them, and Wilson's letter stating that in his numerous appearances before Carswell "there was not a single instance in which
he was ever rude or discourteous to me" had been endlessly
cited, in the Senate and out, on Carswell's behalf. In any event,
Cranston's staff collected what information it could find on
short notice—some of it inaccurate, such as the allegation that
the Administration could fire Wilson if he refused to sign the
letter, whereas actually he was protected under Civil Service
regulations. Then Cranston compounded this sloppy staff work
by failing to ask Wilson if he would substantiate what he had
told Cohen, on the ground that it would be unfair to pressure
the man as the other side had.

At a well-attended press conference on March 30th, Cranston revealed the Wilson story, but when reporters called Wilson he immediately denied it and said that although he had
been "assisted" in drafting the letter, Cranston's charges were
"absolutely untrue." Three hours later, Kleindienst and Rehnquist held a press conference, too, and said that Cranston's
charges were "deliberately misleading" and "absolutely false."
But each time Kleindienst tried to substantiate this, Rehnquist
got up and unwittingly refuted him—as, for instance, when
Kleindienst said that the Department had had nothing to do
with Wilson's letter and then Rehnquist described how he had
visited Wilson at his home to discuss the matter and had
drafted the letter himself. However, this sort of contradiction
received far less coverage and attention than Wilson's denial.

Afterward, several senators were believed to have been so
angered by what appeared to be a vicious smear that they
were tempted to vote for Carswell. Cook was thought to be
one of them, but he privately denied that the episode had had

that effect on him. "It may have said something about Crans-ton, but it said nothing at all about the man we were con-cerned about—Carswell," he explained. Whatever effect the affair had on the outcome finally, it undeniably left a bad im-pression of Carswell's opponents, who now began to look not just desperate but ruthless.

In the end, Rauh took the responsibility for the debacle. "Wilson came to me first and offered to hold a press conference under the auspices of the Leadership Conference to reveal that the letter was a fake," Rauh said afterward. "I asked him to put the facts in an affidavit, but he refused. So I refused to have anything to do with him. One of the basic rules of legal prac-tice is that if somebody is willing to rat on somebody else, you'd better get a sworn statement or he may rat on you, too. Guys who are on the level will go along, and guys who aren't won't. If he was willing to tell his story to the press, why wasn't he willing to put it in writing? I should have warned the others on our side, but it never occurred to me that anyone with ex-perience—least of all a senator—would get snared." There was doubt in other quarters whether Wilson had intentionally laid a trap for anyone. Instead, these people felt, he had succumbed to internal and external pressures almost concurrently—he wanted to expose Carswell, but when the time came and the risks loomed ahead of him he backed away.

Sellers was less inclined to place the blame for the fiasco on Rauh than on Cranston, who, he felt, was more gentleman than politician. "He should have called Wilson in and told him what he was going to do and bluffed him into going along or being made to look like an Uncle Tom," Sellers explained. "A lot of people in this town want to be neutral about everything. At a time like this, you have to say to them, 'You're not neutral, you're opting for the status quo, and in this case that's bad.'

If Cranston had charged Wilson with betraying his own people to keep a cushy job, he could have driven him into a corner and *made* him tell the truth. You don't win in this game by being polite."

The day after the Cranston press conference, Rauh stopped off at the New Senate Office Building to deliver a letter he had composed, containing twenty points against the nomination, to a senator who was reported to be having difficulty in making up his mind. On the way to his office, Rauh passed the suite occupied by Senator William B. Saxbe, Republican of Ohio, who had been telling everyone that he, too, was uncommitted. Deciding to see what he could do to persuade Saxbe to join the opposition, Rauh went in and found the Senator free and happy to discuss the subject. He showed Rauh a copy of a letter he had written to Mr. Nixon asking whether his continuing silence meant that he no longer fully supported the nomination and suggesting that if he did he might make that known and might also personally answer the charges that had been raised since the hearings. Impressed by Saxbe's concern, Rauh showed him *his* letter, and after reading it carefully Saxbe said, "Great!" and asked if he might show it to the other members of the Wednesday Club when they met for their weekly lunch and political talk the following day. Delighted by the opportunity to have the letter presented by a senator to several senators rather than to present it in person to only one senator, Rauh quickly agreed.

Seven senators attended the Wednesday Club luncheon—Brooke, Case, and Goodell, who had already announced that they would oppose Carswell; Mathias and Schweiker, who indicated that they would, too; Cook, who said, for the first time in front of his colleagues, that he planned at that stage to vote against both recommittal and confirmation; and Saxbe, who wasn't uncommitted after all, having made up his mind a week earlier to support Carswell. The lunch got under way with a discussion of whether recommital was the proper course to take. Cook didn't like the idea, because, he argued, it was nothing more than a sneaking attempt to avoid the issue.

Goodell disagreed. "I don't see any difference between recommittal and an up-or-down vote," he said. "I might prefer the latter as a cleaner and more direct method, but since some senators feel easier, politically speaking, about recommittal as a way to kill the nomination, I don't care about procedure. The point is to kill the nomination."

Saxbe tried to argue the others out of their stand against Carswell, and then he presented Rauh's letter—not, as Rauh had expected, to support the opposition but, instead, to support the nomination. "If this is the best the opposition can come up with, you can't vote against Carswell," Saxbe said, and threw the letter down before them.

After reading the letter, several of those present agreed that Rauh's case was not as compelling as it might have been, because it attempted to cover too much ground. To give it the concentrated force it lacked, Goodell presented three points instead of twenty—that Carswell had a lamentable record when it came to civil rights, civil liberties, and honesty. Then Case said that a fourth point, which he felt was more important than all the others together, was that the nation was racked by tremendous social upheavals, particularly racial discord, and that moderate black leaders had to be convinced that the system could be made to work on their behalf. "If we accept Carswell, they'll never listen to us again," he said.

Saxbe's letter to the President had been discussed at the White House several days earlier—as a matter of fact, even before it was written. During a breakfast meeting between the President and Republican leaders in Congress, one participant asked whether it might not be wise for Mr. Nixon to make a strong public statement on Carswell's behalf to rally public support and thereby to bring the troops in the Senate into line behind the Administration. Senator Griffin mentioned that Saxbe was thinking about writing the President a letter asking where he now stood on the nomination, and it was agreed that an answer from the President would be a good way to handle the problem. To expedite matters, Griffin later told Saxbe about the plan, and a lawyer from the White House and two lawyers from the Justice Department got together to prepare an answer to Saxbe's letter, which hadn't arrived yet. They studied the Constitution, "The Federalist," and books on the Constitutional Convention, and then composed a letter that ignored all of them. After assuring Saxbe that the Administration stood behind Carswell all the way, President Nixon's letter went on:

What is centrally at issue in this nomination is the constitutional responsibility of the President to appoint members of the Court—and whether this responsibility can be frustrated by those who wish to substitute their own philosophy or their own subjective judgment for that of the one person entrusted by the Constitution with the power of appointment. The question arises whether I, as President of the United States, shall be accorded the same right of choice in naming Supreme Court Justices which has been freely accorded to my predecessors of both parties.

I respect the right of any Senator to differ with my selection.

It would be extraordinary if the President and 100 Senators were to agree unanimously as to any nominee. The fact remains, under the Constitution it is the duty of the President to appoint and of the Senate to advise and consent. But if the Senate attempts to substitute its judgment as to who should be appointed, the traditional constitutional balance is in jeopardy and the duty of the President under the Constitution impaired.

For this reason, the current debate transcends the wisdom of this or any other appointment. If the charges against Judge Carswell were supportable, the issue would be wholly different. But if, as I believe, the charges are baseless, what is at stake is the preservation of the traditional constitutional relationships of the President and the Congress.

By prearrangement, Saxbe released the President's letter—or what came to be known as the Saxbe letter—on April 1st at a large press conference held in a committee room of the New Senate Office Building. The reaction among senators was uniform indignation. "The Senate doesn't like to do very much, but it doesn't like to be told that it doesn't have the right to do very much," Senator Packwood explained later.

Most members resented the President's attempt to usurp their powers, and just about everyone there agreed with Bayh when he told his colleagues later, "This interpretation is wrong as a matter of Constitutional law, wrong as a matter of history, and wrong as a matter of public policy." To begin with, he went on, the President's insistence—stated several times in the letter—that he alone was empowered to "appoint" justices was a stunning misinterpretation of the Constitution, which stipulates, in Article II, Section 2, "The President . . . shall nominate and by and with the advice and consent of the Senate shall appoint . . . judges of the Supreme Court." In short, the appointive power was to be divided between the President and the Senate; he had the power to name a judge, and the Senate had the power to approve or reject his choice. In "The Federalist," Hamilton described this divided responsibility as a "powerful" and "excellent check" on the President, and added, "If by influencing the President be meant restraining him, this is precisely what must have been intended." Further, President Nixon's peevish claim that he was being denied the right given other Presidents flew in the face of history from the first Administration on down. In 1795, President Washington's choice of John Rutledge as Chief Justice was defeated by the Senate, and over the years twenty-three other nominations to the Court either were rejected or were delayed until they lapsed or were withdrawn because of Senate opposition—the last two being President Johnson's nominations of Abe Fortas and Homer Thornberry.

In answer to the charge raised against Carswell that he had lied under oath to the Judiciary Committee about his part in the golf-club affair, the President presented the same defense that Senator Cooper had—namely, that Carswell had first erred about the golf-club incorporation but had subsequently corrected himself; nothing was said about his firm denials the following day without later retraction. As for the charge of racism, the best that Mr. Nixon could do was to cite the letter that Brooke had used in Carswell's defense before coming out against him—from a shipmate of Carswell's during the Second World War stating that he had always treated the black sailors aboard his ship decently; the President did not mention that the Navy had been firmly segregated at the time.

In an editorial entitled "The President's Trump," the Washington *Evening Star*, which supported Carswell, observed that "Mr. Nixon's initiative in permitting the publication of his letter to Senator Saxbe will put powerful new pressure on wavering senators." The editorial writer was about the only person outside the White House who thought so. In the days following the release of the letter, senator after senator rose on the floor to denounce the President for demanding that the Senate abdicate its responsibilities and give up its rights. Senator Brooke publicly called the letter "shameful," and Minority Leader Scott privately said, "One more stunt like that and Carswell will get two votes."

Various opinions were expressed about the President's motives. One was that he was trying to make the case one of personal loyalty in order to becloud the basic issue. Another was that he was going over the head of the Senate to the public and employing the same kind of distortion that had helped win the Presidency. Still another was that the letter was a clumsy attempt to lay the basis for an attack on the Senate if Carswell was beaten. Whatever the motives, the letter was believed to have shaken some senators who were inclined to support the nominee—among them Margaret Chase Smith, Republican of Maine, who reacted with uncommon fury to any attempts to deny the Senate its rights.

Even Saxbe was put out by the affair. "I thought the President's letter was a poor job," he said in a private conversation afterward. "If it had any effect at all, it was an adverse one. I had hoped he would deal with the questions I raised in my letter. But he dismissed those in one sentence. Then he beat a dead horse, because I had already admitted in my letter that the nomination was his prerogative. I had been hoping for a tight legal brief, but instead I got all this irrelevant stuff."

Despite his feelings about the letter, Saxbe had been willing to be the one to release it because he needed some way to justify his vote back home. Local branches of the major labor unions and civil-rights organizations had stirred up strong sentiment against the nomination in the northern, and more liberal, part of the state, and his mail from Ohio, some four thousand letters in all by the end, was running eight to one against Carswell. When Saxbe held the press conference and gave reporters copies of the President's letter, he also announced that he would vote for the nominee—and pointedly held his nose as he did. "My main reason for endorsing Carswell was that I wanted to protect Senator Scott," Saxbe later explained. "Many of us very much want a new image for the Republican Party. We fought for Scott, and if he loses, all chance for that new image will vanish, because the Hruskas and the Gold-waters will take over. To protect his own position as Minority Leader, Scott *had* to support Carswell. But he wasn't any more enthusiastic about it than I was. My feeling was that if I backed off from Scott on this one and left him standing alone, it would show that he couldn't line up even the moderates and liberals who are supposed to be his faithful followers."

Perhaps Saxbe was able to take this stand because, unlike most other moderate-to-liberal Republicans in the Senate, he did not, as he admitted, share a feeling of reverence toward the Supreme Court. Some of Saxbe's colleagues, whether or not they shared that feeling, saw that it unquestionably had to be reckoned with. For instance, during the debate over Hayns-worth's nomination, Senator Griffin paid a visit to Camp David to beseech the President to withdraw that nomination as an act of statesmanship, and argued that it would revitalize the Republican Party nationally and would increase the President's stature immeasurably, both in the Senate and out. "But he just couldn't get the idea across," a man who was close to Griffin said later. "Nixon simply doesn't understand the gut feeling that the Court is sacred and must not be used for political ends."

In the view of a reporter who had long experience on Capi-tol Hill, both as a journalist and as a senatorial aide, much of the President's attitude could be traced to the influence of Attorney General Mitchell. "The President was a senator for only two years before becoming Vice-President, and has never fully understood the Senate," he said. "And Mitchell has demonstrated time and again that he has no awareness of, or sensitivity to, the senators' political needs, their problems, and most of all, their pride. It's pretty easy to see what must have happened. When even moderates like Griffin urged the President to withdraw Haynsworth's nomination, Mitchell, who had to defend it since he was responsible for it in the first place, must have told Nixon, 'This is not what they claim it is. Actually, it's a political trap, an attempt to get you. If you back down now, you'll never be master in your own house again.' And if the President believed this in the Haynsworth case, the Carswell fight could only have confirmed it in his mind."

Some of the younger Republicans in the Senate felt, as a couple of them admitted in private, that the President was placing his own narrow political advantage above the general good of the nation, and they bitterly resented his attempts to coerce them into going along with him and to impute base motives to them for refusing. With each day, these senators became increasingly convinced that they could not serve their President and the public interest at the same time. "Opposition to the Carswell nomination—however painful it might be for the Republican senators—is a necessary step," David Broder wrote in his Washington *Post* column during this period. "It is necessary for their own political future. It is necessary as a sign to the Administration that there are limits to its compromising of the civil-rights cause. It is necessary as a political corrective to the all-out 'Southern-strategy' advocates. And it is necessary, most of all, if the Republicans are to be a national party capable and worthy of governing this country."

By still another accident of timing, as Saxbe left his press conference another senator entered to take over the room—and the attention of the large gathering of reporters. To their amazement, the new arrival—William B. Spong, Jr., a conservative Democrat from the conservative state of Virginia—went to the lectern and announced that he would vote for recommittal of the nomination. Though surprising at first, Spong's decision made political sense when one considered some recent developments. For one, Senator Harry Byrd, Jr., his senior colleague, had recently broken with the Democrats in Virginia to become an independent, and his departure from the party that his family had controlled inflexibly for two generations left Spong open to a primary challenge by its more conservative wing—a move that Byrd would not have allowed. For another, in 1969 Virginia elected its first Republican governor, a moderate, in more than eighty years, and it was expected that any candidate he chose to run against Spong in the next election would be either a moderate or a liberal. In short, Spong was threatened from both the right and the left. The likeliest solution to his problem, political observers felt, would be for him to attempt to occupy the center and quietly go after the black vote, since

Negro registration in Virginia, as in the rest of the South, had risen so rapidly that black citizens were now believed to hold the balance of power.

This analysis satisfied those who viewed politics as a game in which senators cynically manipulate power blocs by altering their own views to fit the prevailing sentiment. As it happened, though, these facts of political life in Virginia had no effect whatever on Spong, who, probably more than any other member of the Senate, decided the issue on its merits, despite the excruciating pressures on him. "If those factors had weighed with me, I would have voted against Haynsworth, too," he pointed out in the course of a conversation on this subject. "Actually, I was unhappy to vote against Carswell." What made Spong unhappiest was the realization that he would not simply be voting against a nomination but would be subjecting a man to the worst kind of public scorn and humiliation. Next in importance for Spong was his desire to see a conservative Southerner on the Court. These factors pushed him toward an endorsement, but then Carswell's record on the bench pulled him back.

In time, the push-and-pull created such an agonizing dilemma for Spong that he nearly became ill. "He was supercharged, really highly tense over this in a way that I had never seen him before," a friend remarked later. To complicate matters, outside pressures were almost as unendurable as inner pressures—demands from close friends and large campaign contributors that he endorse Carswell; thousands of letters, many of them vituperative and obscene; and, finally, six threats to assassinate him if he opposed Carswell. At that point, Spong took his family to their home outside Norfolk for a rest and a chance to think things over.

Spong took with him the hearing record; the two Columbia

Law School studies showing Carswell's extraordinarily high reversal rate while on the bench; descriptions of the seventeen civil- and human-rights cases in which he had been not only reversed but reversed unanimously; an unedited, free-swinging copy of the minority report of the Judiciary Committee hearings on the nomination; several of Carswell's oponions on federal tax cases that had been recommended by two fellow-Southerners who had recently held high positions in the government—Louis F. Oberdorfer, former Assistant Attorney General of the Tax Division in the Department of Justice, and Mortimer M. Caplin, former head of the Internal Revenue Service, both of whom had visited Spong and urged him to oppose Carswell, only to be told that he could not accept anyone else's judgment on so grave a matter but would have to review all the evidence himself; and, finally, a batch of Carswell's opinions on contract-law cases.

The Senator was deeply impressed by the Columbia study and by the seventeen unanimous reversals. "Then I read the hearings, and concluded that Carswell had been evasive, as charged," Spong recounted later. "After that, I spent a couple of days reading some of his opinions." Several of these were the tax-case opinions sent to him through Oberdorfer and Caplin, but most of them dealt with contract cases, which had been Spong's specialty in his private law practice before he entered the Senate. On the basis of these, he concluded that he could have written better opinions as a first-year law student, and when he took them to a law firm in the building where he had his home office and asked some friends for their appraisal, they concurred.

"But I felt that none of these things, in themselves, were sufficient reason to vote against him," Spong went on. "I felt that he ought to have a chance to straighten out his evasive testimony, to explain these cases and Tuttle's withdrawal, which had also affected me, and that it would be best to reopen the hearings and ask him back. When charges were made against Fortas and he refused to reappear and answer them, that turned me off and I voted against him. When charges were made against Haynsworth and he came back and explained to my satisfaction what had happened, I voted for him. My support for recommittal was not a maneuver to kill the nomination. If Carswell had cleared up the questions that bothered me, I would have been delighted to vote for him. But as it stood his testimony just wasn't satisfactory."

Although Spong did not reveal whether he intended to vote up or down on confirmation if the recommittal motion failed, his aides, who firmly opposed Carswell, were convinced that he would vote no—as in fact he did. Of course, everyone in the opposition was delighted by Spong's arrival—probably no one more than Fulbright, who now had some protection against the expected charge that he was a traitor to the South. Spong, on the other hand, could take no comfort from his alliance with Fulbright, whose stand against the war in Vietnam made him a traitor to the entire country in the eyes of the hawkish residents of Virginia.

While Spong's announcement offset the Saxbe letter, Senator Cook offset Spong the same day by announcing that he intended to oppose recommittal. This created consternation in the anti-Carswell camp, because it suggested that Cook might also support confirmation. Actually, Cook had already made up his mind to vote against Carswell in the end, as he had told those at the Wednesday Club lunch, but he didn't want to reveal it publicly and provoke howls of protest back home. However, he had told the White House where he stood, and asked to be left alone. For a time, he was, apparently because the staff there realized how hard he had worked for them in leading the fight for Haynsworth, and because they knew that Cook's constituents would keep up the pressure on him anyway.

Although Kentucky is a border state, it is intensely proud of its Southern heritage—rather like a man whose uncertainty about his forebears makes him a snob—and is deeply conservative in general. Republican county chairmen, the men who get out the vote on Election Day and who tend to be even more conservative than the average voter, could be expected to be infuriated by Cook's vote. If they were sufficiently angry, of course, they might take the step that all incumbents fear the most—a primary challenge the next time around, which divides one's potential supporters and invariably leads many of them to sit out the general election.

But Cook was having trouble with his conscience. In the Haynsworth contest, he had set down standards for a Supreme Court nominee to demonstrate that his support for this one was by no means casual. One standard was that experience on the federal bench was not enough to qualify one for the Court unless it was accompanied by a record of distinction, and now Cook found that he was stuck with it, since Carswell clearly didn't measure up. His opinions were undistinguished, he had mistreated lawyers in his court, and his reversal rate was shocking, Cook concluded. Even in straightforward civil cases—as opposed to controversial civil-rights suits, in which the law was sometimes unclear—his reversal rate was almost twice as high as other judges'. "I tried to figure out how a federal judge could get himself overruled that often," Cook said later. "When you examine Carswell's cases, you have to conclude that really and truly the man must have some hang-up with the doctrine of *stare decisis*—that is, precedent. His failure, or refusal, to follow that rule, which is the basis of our judicial system, proved that he was the opposite of a strict constructionist."

Another factor that weighed heavily with Cook was Judge Carswell's testimony at the hearings, which the Senator, as a member of the Judiciary Committee, followed carefully. "I remember so vividly that on the first day Jim Eastland was reading Carswell's biographical sketch, and asked him if it was correct," Cook recalled. Taking a copy of the hearing record off his desk, he opened it and read the Judge's answer: " 'Yes, Senator, [but] there is one small error in date. My present memory is that my military service should read 8-9-42 instead of 8-27-42, because I entered on active duty with the Navy in South Bend, Indiana, Notre Dame University, on August 9, 1942.' "

Closing the volume, Cook went on, "Now, he remembered that twenty-eight years before he had gone into the Navy on August 9th, not August 27th. But then on the question of the incorporation of the golf club he suddenly didn't remember anything. He had a twenty-eight-year memory, but he couldn't remember that he had seen the incorporation papers the night before. He must have thought, 'I signed some papers on some place that discriminated, and I have to get out of it.' Instead, he should have pointed out that just about every golf club in the country discriminated then and many still do, that it was done in a place where the question never arose, and that, indeed, he had been wrong even so to sign it. If he had done that, he probably would be on the Supreme Court today."

Still another factor that had influenced him, Cook went on, was Goodell's warning on the day when Cook was presiding over the Senate that Carswell might be on the Court for thirty years or more. Finally, the argument made by others that while undistinguished men had been put on the Court in past years, that was no reason they should be now also had carried great weight. "The errors of a legislator in Congress are only for two or six years' duration," Cook said. "Then, if the people don't like what he did, they can recall him. But the errors of a Supreme Court justice can hurt a whole nation and can't be remedied. I couldn't be a party to allowing that and remain in the Senate."

Over the Easter recess, eight members of the Senate left Washington to attend a conference of the Interparliamentary Union in Monaco. Scott was among them, despite the pleas of Bryce N. Harlow, then the President's director of liaison with Congress, that he stay in town during the last crucial days before the vote on Carswell. Scott retorted that if the period wasn't crucial enough to keep the President and the Attorney General from going to Florida, it wasn't crucial enough to keep him from going to Monaco. Kleindienst also made the same plea, and got the same response—in somewhat harsher language. During the conference, however, Scott took advantage of the relaxed and amiable mood of his colleagues to work on a couple of uncommitted members of the official party, while Bayh, who was also on hand, worked on them to cancel Scott's effect.

Scott remained in Monaco until April 4th, two days before the recommittal vote, but Bayh was too worried about what was happening in his absence to stay that long, and returned on April 1st. On his flight back to Washington, he received a message during a refuelling stop that his wife's father had killed her stepmother and himself. When the plane landed in Washington, Keefe, his chief aide, was waiting with a car and

168

immediately drove him home. Mrs. Bayh had decided to stay over in Monaco until the official party left on the fourth, and didn't get word of the murder-suicide until after her husband had departed. By now, she had left, too, and was due in Washington early the next morning. Shaken by the family tragedy and deeply concerned about its effect on his wife, Bayh paced restlessly through the house for a long time, until he decided that he could do nothing about it until she arrived.

With that, he turned his attention to the Saxbe letter, which had been released that afternoon and which Keefe had given him a copy of on the way back from the airport. Although the letter struck Bayh as an absurdly concocted gimmick, he was worried about the effect it might have not on members of the Senate but on the public. Finally, he called Wise, his press officer, to talk it over and to get his views on whether it would be inexcusably bad taste, in view of the circumstances, to make a speech on the subject the following day, Thursday, April 2nd. Wise thought that could be handled by including a line in the speech to the effect that the importance of the issue overrode even the deepest personal concerns, and finally Bayh agreed and said, "O.K., let's go."

Wise telephoned Mode, who had just arrived at Senator Kennedy's home to attend a farewell party for one of his aides, and Mode left for his office at once. Shortly after he joined Wise there, Keefe and his deputy Rees arrived, and the four men worked throughout the night drafting a speech. At 6 A.M., they went home for a couple of hours' sleep, after which they returned to the office, went over the speech with Bayh, had some secretaries type up the draft, and mimeographed copies of it for the press. Although by this time everyone knew about Horsky's meeting with Carswell, the memorandum describing the details hadn't arrived yet. Informed early that morning by Tydings' office that it was expected momentarily, Wise inserted a couple of references to it in the speech so that Tydings would have an opening to engage Bayh in a colloquy on the subject and then put the memorandum into the record.

Apparently, the other side got word that Bayh and Tydings now had Horsky's version of the meeting, for when Bayh finally got the floor, around four o'clock that afternoon, two of Carswell's Republican backers, Senators Gurney and Dole, continually interrupted him to delay Tydings' maneuver until after the press deadline for morning papers, which is normally around four-thirty. To outflank them, Wise gave key reporters copies of the memorandum (which had also been given to all members of the Senate) and copies of the speech, so that they could use them in their stories for the next morning, and promised that both documents would be a part of the record by adjournment time if Bayh and Tydings had to keep the Senate in session all night. To fulfill Wise's promise, they kept the Senate in session until well after nine o'clock. Although the Horsky memo was clearly the more important document, the next day's papers gave far more attention to Bayh's rebuttal of the President's letter to Saxbe.

It is impossible to assess the effect of the Horsky memo on the outcome, but certainly it was not as great as it would have been if Horsky had not temporized so long—until after most of those who were going to vote for Carswell had announced their position and thereby locked themselves in. One known effect, though, was that it gave those of Carswell's backers who were already uneasy about their stand a few bad hours. For instance, Senator Griffin said afterward, "I was bothered by the Horsky memo. For a whole weekend, I gave that a lot of thought."

Some of his aides tried to persuade him that the memorandum was more than enough to justify him in retracting his support, and one of them said later, "He was within a hair of turning around. But the White House had him locked in, and finally he bit the bullet and said he would stay where he was." To justify that, Griffin instructed a lawyer on his staff to draw up a memorandum on the memorandum to show that it did not prove Carswell a liar. Over that weekend, Griffin also talked to Senator Cooper, of Kentucky, and Senator Williams, of Delaware, to see if the Horsky memo had forced them to withdraw their endorsements, which would have made it easier for him to follow the same course. When they replied that they meant to stick with the White House, he saw that he would have to go along with them. "He couldn't leave the kitchen when the heat was on if no one left with him," one of his assistants explained.

Despite his reservations, Griffin returned to the fray with the kind of determination that only a politician can summon under such circumstances, and began working harder than ever to persuade uncommitted colleagues to join Carswell's backers. The first was Senator Prouty, of Vermont, who was eager to support the President but was up for reëlection and was being hounded by critics of the nomination back home. Prouty's opponent was the former governor of Vermont, Philip Hoff, who had been approached by the anti-Carswell lobby in Washington and was now travelling around the state calling Prouty's earlier promise to vote for Carswell the act of a rubber stamp, not a senator. With independent-minded voters like Vermonters, the charge worked, and the mail opposing Carswell, and anyone who voted for him, began pouring into Prouty's office.

Finally, he gave in, or so it seemed, and promised Brooke

that he would vote against Carswell. But now, when Griffin showed him the memorandum on the Horsky memo, Prouty promised to cast his vote for Carswell if it was needed. It appeared that Prouty's strategy was to vote for recommittal once it was sure to lose, which would allow him to tell his constituents that he wanted the matter reëxamined to make sure that the nominee was qualified and was treated fairly. When recommittal failed, he could then vote for confirmation and justify it by saying that the sense of the Senate had been to accept the nominee's credentials. "That was one of our basic mistakes—counting on Prouty," an outside lobbyist said later. "We put too much work in and too much emphasis on him. We should have known all along that he would go whichever way the strongest wind blew."

There was also some doubt about the firmness of a promise elicited from Senator Thomas J. Dodd, Democrat of Connecticut, to oppose confirmation. Not long before, the Justice Department had announced that it was dropping its case against Dodd for allegedly misusing campaign funds and misreporting his income, and many people concluded that this decision was half of a deal, the other half being Dodd's guarantee that he would support the Administration when it needed him. In the Haynsworth case, for instance, Dodd abstained on the first roll call, and then, when it was clear that the nomination was defeated, he cast his vote against it. He had voted for Carswell in the Judiciary Committee and showed every sign of planning to vote for him on the floor until one of his opponents in the forthcoming primary race in Connecticut, the Reverend Joseph Duffey, national chairman of the A.D.A., and local labor unions began going after him, whereupon Dodd reaffirmed his promise to oppose Carswell on the final vote.

As the date for the vote drew near and the Administration

discovered the extent of the trouble it was in, panic ensued. To counter the effect of the Horsky memo, Deputy Attorney General Kleindienst enlisted the help of judges on District Courts in the Fifth Circuit, and persuaded fifty of the fifty-eight who were on the bench and seven of the thirteen who had retired to endorse Carswell by way of another telegram. In the press and in the Senate, Kleindienst's maneuver was put down as outright intimidation. Whatever the impropriety of his efforts, there could be no doubt about the impropriety of the judges' lobby, for the Judicial Conference, which is made up of federal judges representing all eleven circuits, specifically forbids any political activity by any federal judge for any reason. One judge who was charged with having ignored that was the highest of them all—Chief Justice Warren E. Burger. Although the Chief Justice has angrily denied the charge that he lobbied among several senators to get their votes for Carswell, at least one of them still asserts that he did.

A number of Republican senators observed that they had never seen such incompetent liaison work by an Administration as there was in the Haynsworth case—until the Carswell nomination. In at least one instance, the lines of communication broke down completely in the latter fight. Senator Mathias had been out of the country on Senate business during the Carswell hearings, and since he was a member of the Judiciary Committee, he felt obliged to read the record of the hearings when he got back. Afterward, he was dissatisfied, mainly because he had not had a chance to assess Carswell in person. "All my instincts were directed toward justifying a vote for Carswell," he said later. "I felt that another fight over the Court after Haynsworth was harmful to the Court, to the President, to the Senate, to the Republican Party, and to the country, and I didn't want to be the one who caused that harm if the vote was close, as everyone expected. But as I went into the record and the newspaper reports, I found it more and more difficult to reconcile myself to the nomination. Finally, I asked to meet Carswell."

Mathias made his request to Hruska, and, when nothing happened, to Gurney, and, when nothing happened, to John Dean, the Justice Department's liaison man, who passed it on to Kleindienst. Still nothing happened. Perhaps Kleindienst decided that since Mathias had opposed Haynsworth, he would undoubtedly oppose Carswell and merely wanted to demonstrate to his constituents that he had done everything he could to bring himself to vote for the nominee. If this was the case, Kleindienst ignored one obvious indication that Mathias hadn't made up his mind. "If I had, I wouldn't have asked for a meeting, which was bound to be painfully embarrassing for both Carswell and me," he pointed out.

"Anyway, we were getting down to the wire, and I was becoming increasingly distressed, particularly about Carswell's abominable record on the bench," Mathias continued. "I was worried about the terrible position Scott was in, and wanted to help him if I could. I talked to Cooper, and he argued that Carswell was being held to unreasonable standards, but I couldn't see that. Finally, on April 1st, I renewed my request for a meeting, this time in writing, and sent it to the Justice Department. I never got an answer. That was unprecedented in something as critical as this, where one vote really mattered. I didn't hear from a single person in the executive branch— not from the President, not from the Attorney General or his Deputy, not from anyone lower down—even though I had asked for information and guidance." Finally, Mathias mentioned this to Gurney, who was stunned by the Administration's bumbling, and he called the White House and demanded that it make amends. Almost immediately, Mathias got a call from an aide there who offered to have Carswell flown up from Florida for a meeting with him the night before the vote. Mathias turned down the offer. "I told him that clandestine midnight meetings on judgeships were not in our tradition," he recalled afterward. "Obviously, a meeting under such strained conditions could not have been helpful."

Once the Administration realized that if it lost on the motion to recommit the nomination it would, unlike the opposition, have no second chance, it let fly with everything in its arsenal. By the day before the recommittal vote, the mood in the White House was buoyant, and the press secretary confidently announced that, with four senators expected to be absent, the vote would be fifty to forty-six against the motion. Unknown to the White House, Bayh fully agreed with its forecast of victory and estimated its winning margin would be even larger. Also unknown to the White House, he had given up any hope of recommitting the nomination and, in a secret tactical switch, had turned his attention to the final vote, which the White House, in its frantic concern about recommittal, was ignoring.

Late in the week before the first vote—set for Monday, April 6th—Bayh had concluded that his side would probably lose that because of all the pressures applied by the Administration. He discussed this with Mansfield, who suggested that he might have a better chance if he dispensed with the recommittal motion and moved to take a vote on confirmation in its place. After thinking that over, Bayh finally disagreed, on the ground that many senators who wanted to see Carswell lose also wanted to vote for him in some way—in the case of Republicans, to soothe the President and, in the case of Democrats, to soothe those of their constituents who were for Carswell—and that if the recommittal motion was dropped that would close the door to any token support. No sooner had Bayh made this point than he discovered the solution to his problem—allowing these senators to meet their political needs by releasing them from their commitments to vote for recommittal as long as they kept their commitments to vote against confirmation.

"It was one of those split-second decisions," Bayh said later. "I saw that the Administration had assumed that the recommittal and confirmation votes would be pretty much the same. In its panic, the White House had pursued a policy of overkill to win on recommittal, and I realized that we could use this to undercut it on the final vote."

To carry out the new strategy, Bayh, Brooke, Kennedy, Tydings, and Hart quietly let the others on their side know that it was all right to vote as they pleased on Monday if they voted against confirmation on Wednesday. The shift in strategy was an amazingly well-kept secret, and the White House staff members, blindly pursuing their course, stumbled into the trap. In an attempt to assure victory on the recommittal motion, they went after four key votes those of Fong, Dodd, Packwood, and Percy—and won them with what should have seemed suspicious ease.

"That meant the White House had the Monday vote sewed up," Bayh's aide Rees recalled later. "By then, we were delighted to let them expend all their steam on that, because, although the White House didn't know it, those four men had promised to be with us on Wednesday. That gave us forty-seven votes to forty-five for Carswell on the Wednesday vote. Four senators would be absent, and four more were unknown quantities. If we kept Quentin Burdick, of North Dakota, who seemed to be leaning our way, it would be forty-eight. If Cook, Prouty, and Mrs. Smith all went with the Administration, that would make it a tie, which, of course, the Vice-President would break in favor of the nominee. But while the White House needed all three to win, we needed only one to give us the magic number—forty-nine."

It was generally assumed, however, that these three Republicans would vote alike, in order to protect themselves and each other by creating a margin that they could take refuge in. Otherwise, of course, the one who cast the deciding vote would be open to attack, whichever way he or she cast it, by political opponents at home. One small bit of encouragement about the way one of these three was leaning turned up on the Sunday before the final vote. That afternoon, Tydings and Gurney engaged in a televised debate on the nomination, and as soon as it ended Mrs. Smith telephoned Tydings at the studio to congratulate him on his compelling presentation.

The recommittal vote was set for one o'clock Monday afternoon, and shortly before the roll was called, disaster nearly befell the anti-Carswell cause. Bayh happened to run into Senator Burdick, and learned that through an oversight no one had told him about the new strategy. Burdick was one of those who felt they had to vote once for Carswell, and he was still planning to vote for recommittal and, if that failed, for confirmation. Stunned to learn this, Bayh hastily told him that the plans had been changed, and asked him to switch his votes around. Burdick listened to his plea, nodded as if to indicate that he would go along, but refused to commit himself openly. To a degree, his was the key vote that afternoon, and when he cast it against recommittal, Bayh and Brooke turned and grinned at each other, for now it was clear that he would be with them on the final vote. Another senator who was watched closely that afternoon was Prouty. As expected, he abstained the first time the roll was called, and then, when it was clear that the motion had lost, he voted for it. By this time, the vote was anticlimatic, except that the final tally—fifty-two to forty-four against the motion—showed that the White House staff couldn't count any better when it won than when it lost.

That also surprised no one, and about the only unexpected occurrence took place during the debate preceding the vote, as Senator Aiken rose and put in question his reputation for sagacity by delivering a one-sentence speech on behalf of the nomination: "We need some law and order and to stop apologizing to every criminal." Afterward, a Republican colleague shook his head in disbelief and said, "George must have got a new speechwriter—Strom Thurmond."

In the course of the debate, Scott casually remarked to Mansfield that the anti-Carswell forces now clearly had the votes to defeat the nomination on Wednesday. Nodding, Mansfield went over to Bayh and suggested that after the recommittal motion failed he move to take an up-or-down vote on the nomination not two days later but two hours later. Bayh liked the idea, and as soon as the votes were counted and the result was announced he rose and asked for a unanimous-consent agreement to take a final vote at three o'clock that afternoon.

Hruska was so flabbergasted by the proposal—a clear sign that Scott hadn't mentioned it to *him*—that he jumped up and shouted, "The Nebraska from Senator objects!" The objection may have been backwards—it was later reversed in the *Congressional Record* by one of Hruska's aides, since senators are allowed to edit their remarks on the floor—but it was enough to kill the motion.

After the session broke up, Hruska confidently assured reporters that the Administration would win the contest on Wednesday by at least three, and perhaps four, votes. At lunch in the Senate dining room a little later, Brooke stopped at Hruska's table and twitted him about the remark, saying, "Roman, you can count, and so can I. If you had the votes, you would have agreed to Birch's motion on the spot."

That afternoon, everyone's attention turned to Cook, Prouty, and Mrs. Smith. Although Cook had been in the Senate only a couple of years and wasn't well known there, he was regarded as a man of honor, and Brooke considered his promise as being firm. However, Cook was also known for his exceedingly complicated nature, and there was always the possibility that the White House would find some way of appealing to a part of it that others were unaware of. Prouty, it was assumed, would take the least thorny path of political expediency. And, as usual, no one had any idea what Mrs. Smith might do. At the age of seventy-two, with twenty-two years in the Senate, Mrs. Smith is known, variously, as "the grand old lady from Maine," "the Senate's most independent member," and "the best argument against women's liberation in town."

Over the years, Mrs. Smith has carefully nurtured a reputation for fiercely resenting any pressure exerted on her, whatever the motive and whatever the issue. Her unapproachable stand has long been highly popular with her Down East constituents and rather unpopular with many of her colleagues who, unlike her, have polyglot constituencies and have to bargain and compromise endlessly to hold on to their seats. Mrs. Smith plays her role with the skill of a great actress. When an issue of moment is before the Senate, she invariably holds off announcing her decision, and then when the time comes for the vote she demurely enters the Senate chamber, which falls utterly silent as her name is called, and in a small, soft voice she makes her will known. In the view of one aide who has worked on the Hill for a dozen years, "Maggie is not so interested in what line she delivers, as long as she can deliver it from stage center."

Just about everyone was afraid to give any appearance of violating the sanctity of Mrs. Smith's independence openly, but now a couple of moves were made to violate it covertly. Toward the end of the contest, Sellers, who had worked so hard to bring Fong around, happened to mention to Bayh's staff that if Carswell was confirmed he would be the justice who oversaw the First Circuit, which took in Maine, and would have jurisdiction over stays of execution, contested federal actions in the region, and other legal affairs that would be of concern to a politician with both local and national responsibilities. Sellers was asked for a memorandum on this, and when it arrived Bayh's press officer, Wise, telephoned the Boston office of the A.P., where the news was rejected by the acting night editor, who told him that it was "a Washington story," and then the Boston *Globe*, where the assistant managing editor was very interested—and rather put out that his staff hadn't thought of it. Wise dictated the information contained in Sellers' memorandum, and a story on it appeared on the front page of the next day's edition. That was said to have impressed Mrs. Smith, who had been unaware that Carswell would have such an effect on her domain if he reached the Court.

A surprising number of other senators turned out to be unaware of even the latest and hottest news, including the Horsky memo and Tuttle's withdrawal, which were the most important stories of all. When aides to the leaders of the opposition discovered this, they quickly alerted the press, which set out to inform senators who had neglected to inform themselves. For instance, the Washington *Post* ran a lengthy article on the memo's implications, which was believed to have impressed a number of senators who were wavering. Then Hruska, who had a long history of being unable to remain silent when anything he said could only make a bad case worse, wrote the paper an angry and inaccurate letter denying the charges, which prompted the *Post* to run a persuasive point-by-point rebuttal of his claims, and that impressed the undecided senators even more.

It turned out that Mrs. Smith was also unaware of the Horsky memo's meaning, for after the recommittal vote she told Brooke that she was troubled by the charge that Carswell had been less than frank with the Judiciary Committee and wanted to know more about it. Brooke promised to send her some material on it, and called Bayh's office for help. The job fell to Mode, who drew up a four-page document describing the situation in the simplest terms, underlined the relevant passages in the hearing record and placed paper clips on the pages where these appeared, and then appended copies of the affidavits submitted by Tallahassee residents stating that everyone in town who knew anything knew that the golf course was incorporated privately to get around the recent Supreme Court desegregation ruling.

By the time Brooke got the material and sent it on to Mrs. Smith, early the following morning, he was deeply apprehensive, because he had just learned that the President had summoned her to the White House the night before and presented *his* case for Carswell. It was reported that she had refused to tell Mr. Nixon how she would vote, and the next morning, a few hours before the roll was called, she told Brooke that she wouldn't decide until her name came up.

When we agreed to a two-day delay between the votes on recommittal and confirmation, we hadn't thought the latter was important at all," Keefe said later. "Like the Administration, we figured the big vote would be on whether the nomination should be sent back to committee. But when our strategy changed, those two days became nerve-rackingly vital, because the White House was turning on everything it had." One thing it didn't have was any chance to persuade the four senators who had promised to vote against recommittal to vote its way on confirmation, too. Before the Administration saw what was happening, the four publicly stated that they would oppose both recommittal and confirmation. Finally seeing the trap, the White House appealed to them to vote for Carswell on Wednesday, but they pointed out that all they had been asked for was their support on the first vote, and that since they had told their constituents where they stood on confirmation, they couldn't back down now and let it appear that they didn't know their own minds.

The Administration apparently also imagined that Fulbright had merely made a gesture toward his liberal friends in voting for the recommittal motion, and that his vote would be in its column when the motion to confirm the nomination came up. Once again, the White House intelligence system had broken down, because several developments in Fulbright's political life clearly pointed in the opposite direction. For one, in his 1968 Democratic primary campaign against Jim Johnson, a white-supremacist, Fulbright for the first time openly appealed for black votes, because he believed that he couldn't win without them and that the "seggies," who hated him for his stand on the war in Vietnam, would vote against him no matter what he did. Then, at the beginning of 1969, Fulbright was the only Southern senator to support the nomination of Dr. James Allen, a Northern integrationist, as Commissioner of Education, and was one of only three Southerners to support the Voting Rights Act back in March.

While Tydings' arguments against Carswell had impressed Fulbright, probably more important to his thinking was the case made by Dr. Robert Leflar, who had formerly held the deanship of the University of Arkansas Law School, a post that Fulbright had held before becoming president of the university and then senator. Most of the law school's faculty came out against Carswell, and then Leflar, who knew and had supported Haynsworth, flatly told Fulbright that Carswell simply was not fit to sit on the Supreme Court. That, plus the outpouring of protests against the nomination from other law-school deans, jurists, and prominent legal scholars, convinced Fulbright that he had no choice but to join them.

The White House intelligence operators finally got wind of this—several days after everyone else knew it—and set out to recapture the vote they had never had. Their principal tactic was to ask friends and contributors to Fulbright's past campaigns who were indebted to the Nixon Administration —for its slowdown on school desegregation, say, or for government contracts—to demand that he change his mind. But when these people called Fulbright, they were reluctant to demand anything, and made it clear that they were calling only because the White House wanted them to. Of course, that drained off any strength their appeals might otherwise have had.

Still another influence on Fulbright was his wife, who had been astonished and infuriated during the squabble over Haynsworth when Attorney General Mitchell's wife telephoned her and threatened to campaign against Fulbright if he betrayed that nominee. As it turned out, Fulbright voted for Haynsworth, but the threat left his wife so embittered that she let him know she wouldn't mind at all if he came down against Carswell, whatever the reprisals.

Another Southerner, Senator Albert Gore, Democrat of Tennessee, had long stood as one of the few exceptions to the racist mood among Southerners in the Senate, and had voted for almost all of the civil-rights measures that counted. But this year his problem was compounded by the fact that he was up for reëlection and was in graver danger of defeat than ever before in his thirty-two years in Congress, because the President had made his seat the prime target in his Southern strategy and his attempt to take over the Senate. Gore was as resistant to outside influence as Mrs. Smith—but never waved the banner of his independence as she did—and lobbyists on both sides in the Carswell fight were careful not to let their work in Tennessee be visible. Halfway through the contest, they got the impression that Gore had not made an announcement on the Carswell nomination because he had not heard from the labor unions back home. At one of the strategy meetings that were held every few days in Bayh's office, the union representatives were told that they had fallen down on the job, and they immediately mounted an anti-Carswell mail campaign among workers in Tennessee. In all likelihood, the mail had little effect, for Gore must have known that the labor vote would be in his corner as usual. Probably he waited for the mail to come in not so much to be sure before he made a commitment as to make sure that he would be able to call on the unions for help the following fall.

In any event, it was believed that both Fulbright and Gore relied chiefly on Hruska to help them out of any difficulties they could expect from angry voters at home. His astonishing defense of mediocrity provided a likely solution, for now they could tell their constituents that they, too, wanted a Southerner and a strict constructionist on the Court, but not one who wasn't smart enough to deal with the damn Yankees.

Out in Texas, Senator Ralph Yarborough, a liberal Democrat of the old-fashioned populist variety, was also faced with the strongest challenge of his career—a formidable primary contender and, if he got through the primary, a formidable Republican opponent in the fall. The contest over Carswell was largely an underground matter in Texas, for all that mattered to many people there was that he was a Southerner, which to them meant a segregationist. That was seldom mentioned—not nearly as often, for instance, as the prayer-in-the-schools issue, which was entirely aboveground and was being used to great effect against Yarborough, who stood by the Constitutional dictum separating church and state despite the bitter resentment that created at home.

None of those on the anti-Carswell side had any doubt about where Yarborough would stand if he voted as he wanted to. His greatest fear was that if he opposed the nomination he might end up as one of the usual ten or twelve liberals who could be counted on to vote their consciences; if that had been the case, he would have found great difficulty in taking the risk of joining them. Above all, he needed concealment—enough other votes against Carswell to make his own seem common-place. As soon as that happened, he was prepared to vote with them. Yarborough then turned to local labor leaders, who had pressed him to make this choice—after the anti-Carswell labor lobby in Washington had pressed *them*—and asked that they now protect him by convincing the ordinary workingman that Carswell's presence on the Court would be against his interests. But the union heads, whose support has increasingly proved in recent years to be less help than hindrance in political campaigns were more worried about harming themselves among their followers than about Yarborough's harming him-self among his, and they failed to do the job. The final vote on the nomination was due a couple of weeks before the primary election in Texas, and as it approached it became clear that Yarborough would probably lose. No one, it ap-peared, could help him if he voted against Carswell. Even Hruska was of little use, for, as one of Yarborough's closest associates said later, "mediocrity isn't a marketable issue in Texas."

The day before the final vote, the Administration once more demonstrated its capacity for ineptitude by dispatching Eugene Cowen, a White House liaison man with Congress, in search of an anti-Carswell senator who would agree to pair his vote with Senator Karl E. Mundt, a conservative Republican from South Dakota, who had been hospitalized for several months following a severe stroke and who presumably would be in favor of the nomination. The other senators who were going to be "unavoidably absent" were Clinton P. Anderson, Democrat of New Mexico, who had just undergone an operation for glaucoma, and Claiborne Pell, Democrat of Rhode Island, and Wallace F. Bennett, Republican of Utah, both of whom were in the Far East on Senate business. The absence of the four was understood to have no effect on the vote, since two were for Carswell and two were against him.

Pairing is a parliamentary procedure by which votes are recorded but don't count in the final tally—that is, it gives those who are not able to be present when the roll is called a chance to state how they would vote if they were. Anyone who is present and agrees to vote in a pair with someone who isn't present ordinarily does so because he knows that his vote won't matter anyway or because he wants to sidestep, at least formally, an issue that is particularly delicate for him. Of course, in this instance the vote was particularly delicate for half the members of the Senate, and anyone who threw his vote away on a pair would be open to the bitterest criticism from constituents and political enemies. That circumstance aside, Cowen's search was still futile, for Mundt was thought to be almost totally incapacitated, and if a paired vote had been announced in his name several senators would have demanded an official investigation to make sure that it hadn't been cast by one of Mundt's or the White House's aides.

While Cowen was frantically looking for someone to pair with Mundt, others on the White House staff were frantically trying to persuade Senator Howard W. Cannon, Democrat of Nevada, to come over to the Administration's side. Nevada is a deeply conservative state, and its residents tend to be most conservative of all on the law-and-order issue, focussing a great deal of resentment against the Supreme Court's rulings on the rights of criminal defendants. (Probably nowhere in the country is the breakdown of order more difficult to attribute to the Court than in Nevada, where the high general crime rate is largely due to legalized gambling, which has brought hordes of organized and unorganized criminals into the state, and where the high murder rate is largely due to the absence of any meaningful gun laws.) Cannon had won his last race by only eighty-four votes, and since he was up for reëlection in the fall, there was every reason for him to share whatever of his constituents' strongest views he could. He had chosen, above all, to share their views on the Supreme Court.

"Frankly, I would like to see the Court more conservative, so Carswell seemed fine at first," he explained later. "I felt that the President was entitled to a man with any philosophy he wants. But in time it became clear that his choice wasn't an outstanding jurist. I was influenced by the failure of Carswell's colleagues to support him. Then came Hruska's statement defending mediocrity, which made it much easier for all of us to oppose the nominee. Then came the reversal rate. Then came the Horsky memo. Still, I had a lot of hard decisions to make and was subjected to a lot of pressure from both sides. Anyway, I was on the fence until the day of the vote." To bring him down on the Carswell side, an Administration spokesman called and promised that if he voted for the nominee he would get "a free ride" in the fall—that is, a weak Republican opponent.

In the last days before the vote, the White House also worked hard on Senator Burdick by promising that *his* opponent in the fall in North Dakota would be left on his own if Burdick voted right, but that President Nixon and Vice-President Agnew would campaign for the challenger if Burdick voted wrong. Confident that his opponent would be too weak to benefit from such help, Burdick held fast—as he undoubtedly would have in any case.

Then the Administration turned to Senator Schweiker, of Pennsylvania, whose defection from both the President and Scott it found impossible to believe. In one of the crudest miscalculations of the entire battle, the Administration released to a reporter from *Newsweek* a list of the people it had called in Pennsylvania to bring pressure to bear on Schweiker, among them large campaign contributors, county chairmen, mayors, state legislators, federal judges, and personal friends. This clumsy attempt to browbeat Schweiker infuriated him. He was also bewildered by the move, and said later, "If they knew anything at all about me, they wouldn't have been so stupid, because it was bound to boomerang."

When an anti-Carswell lobbyist heard about the maneuver, he laughed and said, "They figured that since this sort of gambit works with Scott it should work with Schweiker, too. Of course, they forgot one elementary point—Scott is up for re-election and Schweiker isn't."

While the Administration's repeated blunders created a good bit of amusement, some people were alarmed by its persistent inability to understand what was going on—a failure that could be calamitous in an international crisis, for instance. Senator Cook, who visited the White House on both Monday and Tuesday before the vote and was frequently telephoned by aides there when he wasn't on the premises, was reported to have come away convinced that none of them could believe anyone in Congress could ever behave in anything but a purely political way. In Cook's view, it was far too late to expect a last-minute switch by a senator with the least notion of his public responsibility. "I don't think that someone who deals with an issue as serious as the elevation of a man to the Supreme Court can accept the idea that he is open to a switch at a crucial time," he said. "It just isn't that fluid once you've studied and thought about it."

Above all, the Administration's apparent conviction that in politics there could be no principle led it to persistently overestimate the effects of pressure on members of the Senate and to ignore their consciences. "There's probably not a man here who is unaware that in our system one Supreme Court justice is equal to eleven senators," an aide to a Republican senator who was *not* close to the White House said later. "Those who were most concerned about Carswell's fitness to serve on the Court were also aware that he would probably be there a lot longer than most of them will be here, and might do irreparable damage to our country. Even more important, as these men viewed it, was the likelihood that Carswell's confirmation might well be the final blow for the blacks, and that if the Senate turned its back on them their moderate leaders would lose any chance of keeping them within the system."

Late one evening, after a long day of acrimonious exchanges between opposing sides in the debate, Senator Hart took the floor, and, in an extemporaneous speech that was probably the most eloquent statement made throughout the entire contest, recounted how impressed he had been by a letter he had just received from a constituent who was concerned about that danger. More than the usual number of senators were present in the chamber, and they fell silent as Hart proceeded to read part of the letter: "'Over the past fifteen years, we have been engaged in a slow, often painfully faltering, process of redressing injustices committed against our Negro population during the past three centuries. Not only is this crucial undertaking incomplete, its eventual success remains seriously in doubt. To name at this time to any high-level federal post a man whose views on racial equality are open to question would be a grave error. To make such an appointment to the nation's highest tribunal—the very institution in which most black citizens have, plausibly, deposited maximum confidence —would bring incalculably tragic consequences.'"

Putting down the letter, Hart went on to remind his colleagues of what Mr. Nixon had said when he accepted his Party's nomination for the Presidency: "'Let those who have the responsibility for enforcing our laws, and our judges who have the responsibility to interpret them, be dedicated to the great principles of civil rights.'" And, finally, Hart repeated Carswell's 1948 campaign statement: "'I yield to no man, as a fellow-candidate, or as a fellow-citizen, in the firm, vigorous belief in the principles of white supremacy, and I shall always be so governed.'" After that, Hart went on to point out that Haynsworth had been rejected because of his economic conflicts-of-interest on the bench, and observed that the case now before the Senate was "not portfolio but people." If Haynsworth was turned down and Carswell was confirmed, he added, there would be no doubt in the minds of black people where the Senate stood when *their* interests were at stake.

Then, pausing to look around the chamber at his colleagues, who had been listening intently, Hart concluded by asking, "Is it prudent or right or wise or responsible to place on the one Court to which we appeal to the black American to turn for relief of injustice a man over whom will hang that kind of statement? . . . What we were is part of what we are, and what we are tonight is part of what we will be. If I were a black American, would I ever be able to convince myself that that little part of G. Harrold Carswell, in his pledge always to support white supremacy, might not be a part of him tonight and tomorrow when I am in front of him? And in that sense . . . is it prudent to put on the Supreme Court a man who, having made that statement, we must now say of him to twenty million black Americans, 'Oh, he did not mean it,' or, 'Honest, he has changed. Have faith in the system.'?"

Bayh had flown out to Houston to keep a speaking engagement before the Texas League of Women Voters the afternoon before the final vote, and when he returned the next morning and went to his office, around nine o'clock, Keefe and Rees filled him in on the latest rumors that were swirling about the Capitol. He calmly shrugged off the stories that Carswell would win, and said that the vote would be fifty-one to forty-five against the nomination. Rees, who believed that forty-nine votes were the most they could hope for, remarked that the Senator was obviously very tired, and suggested that he get some sleep. But Bayh had another pressing family matter to attend to; his father had been hospitalized with an angina attack the day before in Washington, while Bayh was in Texas, so he set off for the hospital, saying that he would meet them on the floor of the Senate at ten-thirty, shortly after the beginning of the three-hour debate that was to precede the vote.

Another aide, Mode, rode with him to the hospital and then to the Capitol, and went over with him all the papers he might need, including a secret memorandum that Bayh had asked him to prepare in the event of a tie vote. The first part was entitled "Scenario for Tie Vote on Carswell." It began, *"Upon Announcement of Tie Vote—*rise trying loudly to raise question of order. This fails since can't be raised until division complete (Rule XX, Sec. 1). . . . *When the Vice-President Votes—*rise shouting 'I raise the point of order that the Vice-President cannot vote to advise and consent to a nomination to the Supreme Court.'" The memorandum went on to suggest what to do "if he ignores point of order," "if we're lucky," "if he's on the ball," "after the parliamentary hassle," "if they move to reconsider," and finally "if they move to notify the President immediately." Attached to this document was a three-page speech presenting the case against the right of the Vice-President to cast the deciding vote in such a situation.

In short, the argument was that while the Vice-President's implicit Constitutional authority to break a tie vote in a legislative matter or a nomination to the executive branch was well established, his authority to break a tie in nominations to the federal courts was not. The argument was more ingenious than legally sound, but no one expected it to prevail anyway. It was merely part of a parliamentary maneuver by which Bayh might force the Vice-President to delay his tie-breaking vote. It that worked, then Bayh was to filibuster until Andrew Biemiller, the A.F.L.-C.I.O. lobbyist who had been working against the nomination from the start, could fly out to New Mexico in a chartered jet, snatch Senator Anderson out of his sickbed, and fly him back to Washington to cast the deciding vote against Carswell.

Early on the morning of April 6th, Senator Cook telephoned Mrs. Smith and told her that he was going to vote against Carswell, and that since she and Prouty held the other swing votes, he thought they should know what he would do when the roll was called. She thanked him, and remarked that perhaps her vote wasn't needed then. Cook also talked to Prouty, who said that he, too, intended to vote against the nomination. Then Cook telephoned the White House and told them what he intended to do. To soften the blow, he mentioned that apparently they could now get Mrs. Smith's vote, and added that with Prouty's vote, which everyone knew was available if needed, the White House would have to find only one other vote to create a tie. With that, Harlow and his staff once again set to work—or, as others saw it, they once again panicked.

On Harlow's orders, Cowen got on the line to Schweiker and told him that Mrs. Smith had promised to support the nomination, that Prouty would too, and that now his own vote was the one that counted, the one that could save the President from a humiliating defeat. Schweiker hadn't announced his intention to vote against confirmation, because he believed that would bring immediate demands from Pennsylvania for Scott to take the same course. By not revealing his intention, Schweiker also made the decision appear more difficult than it was—another maneuver to protect Scott as much as he could. Apparently, the White House mistook these adroit precautions for indecision, and decided to apply all the pressure it could. In any case, the call left Schweiker reeling. "The President clearly was making personal loyalty the final test," he said later. "I knew that whatever the vote was in the end, it would really be a one-vote decision, because the balance of the margin would simply be made up of the votes cast after the swing man cast his. That made my responsibility deeper than ever when I realized that my one vote could turn it around."

As it happened, Senators Percy and Mathias got identical calls from the White House—a tactic known in the political trade as "pancaking," or, as Mathias called it, "a case of multiple uniqueness." Percy was in a quandary about which side he should vote with. He had campaigned for the Senate in 1966 on a liberal platform, but much of his support in that election came from voters in the conservative southern portion of Illinois, who were convinced that he had to appear liberal in order to beat the noted liberal incumbent, Paul Douglas; they were also convinced that Percy would be a different man once he got into office, and were embittered to discover that he voted almost as liberally as he talked. Illinois was also strong Nixon country, and the Republican governor, Richard B. Ogilvie, a Nixon stalwart, had threatened Percy with a primary opponent in 1972 if he let the President down this time. On the other side, Brooke kept after Percy following the recommittal vote, and pointed out that whatever the leaders of the party in Illinois said now, they would discover later on that they needed him more than he needed them. In the end, Percy agreed with Brooke's reasoning.

As for Mathias, he had decided to follow his conscience and vote against Carswell. "My decision created hideous political problems for me at home," he said afterward. "Orthodox Republicans, Democrats who voted for me last time on the ground that a Republican would be more pro-South than a Democrat, and many of my personal friends were aghast at my even thinking about voting against the nomination. They were bound to be furious with me when I did. Of course, that could mean a primary opponent next time around and far less in the way of money and help."

But Schweiker was undoubtedly the most distressed of the three who heard from the White House. "Half an hour before the time for the vote, I still had the problem," he recalled later. "Finally, I forced myself to put aside the responsibility of what one vote could do and tried to judge the issue solely on its merits. I had to convince myself in the few remaining minutes that the one-vote idea was irrelevant to my decision. Once I did that, I saw that in all conscience I had to vote no."

Shortly after eleven o'clock, as the final debate on the nomination was in progress, a woman on Brooke's staff told him that she had just learned from the Minority Leader's office that Mrs. Smith had promised the White House her vote. Brooke began looking for Mrs. Smith at once, but it was over an hour before he found her—at lunch in the Senate dining room, just below the Senate chamber, where Senators Cooper and Tydings were engaged in a bitter floor debate about which side had misrepresented Carswell's record. Brooke reminded her that she had told him she would not decide how she would cast her vote until the time came, and asked if it was true, as the White House was claiming, that she had promised to vote for Carswell. She colored, and he hastily added that he had no intention of trying to influence her one way or the other but thought she should know what was happening if indeed she had not made up her mind yet.

Furious at this development, Mrs. Smith went to a telephone, called Harlow, and demanded to know whether he had told other senators she would support the nomination. Harlow tried to sidestep the question, whereupon Mrs. Smith cursed him, slammed down the receiver, and hurried off to the Senate chamber. She went first to Schweiker and asked if he had got such a call, and he assured her that he had. Then she asked Mathias the same question and got the same answer. With that, she went to her desk and sat, tight-lipped, waiting for the roll call to begin.

At a little before one o'clock, two deep buzzer signals—for a quorum call, the preliminary step to a vote—rang throughout the Senate office buildings across the broad lawns of the Capitol to summon those who were not already on the floor or in the cloakrooms. Even elevator boys and the greenest secretaries knew what this particular signal meant, and everyone watched solemnly as senators, followed by batteries of aides, emerged from their offices and walked down the long marble-floored corridors toward the elevators and thence to the subways connecting the office buildings to the Capitol. The Senate chamber was more crowded than anyone could remember seeing it. The galleries were packed with the lobbyists who had fought for and against the nomination, and with Senate assistants and secretaries. The rear of the Senate floor was jammed with rows of aides who had floor passes, congressmen who had taken advantage of the exchange of floor privileges between the Senate and the House, and even a couple of former senators, who retain for life the right to visit the Senate. Outside, the corridors were filled with people who hadn't been able to get inside.

Promptly at one o'clock, a single buzzer rang, signalling

the beginning of a roll-call vote. The first four votes were for Carswell, and then the clerk called, in his deep, resonant voice, "Mr. Bayh," and Bayh had the privilege of casting the first negative vote. Echoing his "No" with a long-drawn-out "No-o-o-o," the clerk resumed the roll, and it stood at nine to four in favor of the nomination when he called, "Mr. Cook." Cook faced the front of the chamber, where Vice-President Agnew was seated as presiding officer, and thundered, "No!" A gasp rose from the audience, for most of those on hand knew that this was the crucial vote, unless the White House had managed to break loose someone who had been thought to be locked in with the opposition. Then some of the votes that might have been changed—Dodd, Fong, and Fulbright—came in quick succession, and as each of them called out, "No," another gasp rose from the audience. When the clerk got to Prouty and he registered a "No," applause burst out briefly, but the Vice-President quickly silenced it with a rap of his gavel. Then Schweiker voted his conscience, and everyone turned to watch Mrs. Smith, who was seated impassively, wearing her usual red rose. The clerk called her name, and she answered, in a quiet, utterly unemotional voice, "No." That brought a roar of approval from the galleries and more applause, for her vote made twelve Republicans opposed—the number necessary to defeat the nomination.

At the end of the first roll call, the tally stood at forty-six to forty-four against the nomination; six senators either had not voted the first time around or had not reached the chamber in time to answer when their names were called. But there was no question about the outcome now, since it would take four votes for Carswell out of the six to produce a tie, and three of the six were firmly opposed. In the end, five of the six went against the nomination, and one went for it. Precisely as Bayh had predicted, the final tally was fifty-one to forty-five. When Vice-President Agnew announced the result, the galleries burst into applause, whistles, and shouts, with a scattering of catcalls and boos. Senator Richard B. Russell, the Democratic patriarch from Georgia, who had originally suggested Carswell's name to Senator Gurney, angrily demanded that the galleries be cleared. The Vice-President obeyed, and the guards tried to carry out his order, but by then, of course, everyone was leaving anyway.

Among the aides in the back of the chamber, Flug was laughing and weeping at the same time. "I just can't believe it!" he kept saying. "It's too good to believe."

Congressman John Conyers, who had gone on fighting the nomination throughout the seventy-nine-day period since Mr. Nixon sent Carswell's name to the Senate, was also present on the floor, and when he emerged from the chamber he had an expression compounded of disbelief and delight. "Carswell's defeat is an incredible symbol of how public sentiment can work its will even in this insulated system called Congress," he said when he finally collected himself. "It was a terrific psychological victory to show that the people can still have their way."

Later that day, Senator Cook, the hero or villain of the hour, held a press conference to explain why he had voted against the nomination—principally, he said, because Judge Carswell did not have the support of all the judges on the Fifth Circuit and because his "extraordinarily high reversal percentage" refuted the claim that he was a strict constructionist. Cook also took this opportunity to explain why he had not revealed his position earlier, saying that in light of his leadership in the Haynsworth fight his opposition to Carswell might have influenced others to go along with him and he had not wanted to affect the outcome in any way except by his own vote. "Consequently, I have kept my own counsel and have now cast what I consider to be the most politically dangerous vote of my public career," he added. "I say this because I know that the people of my state are anxious for a Southern judge to be put on the Supreme Court. Well, so am I. I know that our people would like to see a conservative approved for the Court, and so would I. But, most of all, I know the people of Kentucky want an outstanding Southern conservative on the Supreme Court, and so do I. . . . I do not see that man in Harrold Carswell. Therefore, I cast my vote as I did because I could not in good conscience do otherwise."

Afterward, an aide to a Democratic leader of the opposition to Carswell said, "Cook was a pillar of strength. His decision must have been excruciatingly difficult." It was. Knowing that most of his constituents would be enraged by his act and would fail to see that he must have known he would incur their wrath but morally *had* to vote as he did, Cook took a further step to mollify them by recounting how he had finally made up his mind the day before the vote after attending a White House ceremony at which President Nixon awarded twenty-one Medals of Honor posthumously. At the time, Cook explained, "When I came back from the White House, I thought, 'Those were men who did their best and lost their lives.' And all of a sudden I thought that we were going to vote for someone who didn't fulfill the degree of excellence in the legal field that I thought those men deserved."

Most people in Washington dismissed this statement as a piece of sentimental hokum. Harlow, for instance, asked him, "Marlow, are you *serious*?" Cook assured him that he was.

That night, Cook stayed in his office late to catch up on his work, and when he left he ran into a group of Senate aides who were winding up their celebration over Carswell's defeat. He stopped to talk with them for a few moments, and mentioned that one of the influences he had not revealed in his press conference was a letter from a former law partner in Kentucky, who had appealed to him to reject Carswell as the only way to stop the deep discontent among Negroes from bursting into a bloody upheaval. Cook paused thoughtfully, then grinned and added, "I hope they send the Attorney General's name up next, so we can turn him down, too."

S enator Yarborough was beaten in his primary by about a hundred thousand votes out of one and a half million cast, and he was convinced that his stand against Carswell had cost him his seat. News of Yarborough's defeat was received with dismay by most of his fellow-Democrats in the Senate, especially by those who had voted the same way and were also facing reëlection contests. Few were more dismayed than Senator Cannon, who soon learned that instead of the free ride promised by the White House if he supported Carswell he was in for the costliest ride of his political life for opposing him. At the time of the vote, it had appeared that the Republicans would be unable to find a powerful candidate to run against him, because the two strongest Republican figures in Nevada were vying with each other for a crack at the governorship. Now, however, the White House interceded, and Vice-President Agnew, on instructions from the President, persuaded one of them—William Raggio, the district attorney of Washoe County, which includes Reno—to run against Cannon, and promised that both he and the President would campaign for him. Even more unsettling to Cannon was the Republican Party's promise to spend half a million dollars on

Raggio's campaign, an enormous sum for a small state like Nevada. "The Administration has said that it can win a Senate seat at less cost in Nevada than anywhere else in the country," Cannon explained. Of course, he could not hope to raise that kind of money, nor could the Democratic Party in Nevada or the Democratic National Committee, both of which were deeply in debt already. As it turned out, though, Cannon fought a hard campaign—in the opinion of some, abetted by the Vice-President's and the President's intercession, which was resented by the voters—and won by nearly three to two.

It was believed that Minority Leader Scott would be in serious trouble during his reëlection campaign, too, because of his support and vote for Carswell. At the start of the campaign, Scott did his best to soothe his liberal and black constituents by saying publicly, "Perhaps I erred in judgment on the Carswell case." About that time, Carswell was defeated in a Senate primary election in Florida, and Scott took that opportunity to remark publicly that it was "fortunate Florida has not nominated a racist." In the end, Scott won with fifty-two per cent of the vote.

Senator Gore, who had always played the underdog in election campaigns and had won seven terms in the House and three in the Senate, discovered that he was an authentic underdog at last. Although the President unwittingly came to his aid during the primary by threatening to personally campaign against him, thereby showing the independent-minded voters of Tennessee that Gore was in trouble because he was independent, he won that election—but by the narrow margin of thirty thousand votes. That was only a third of what he, and others, felt he needed to beat his Republican opponent in the fall. Toward the close of that campaign, his votes against Haynsworth and Carswell became one of the four main issues his opponent concentrated on. In the end, Gore lost by less than fifty thousand votes out of more than a million cast, and it was believed in his camp that if he had voted in favor of either nominee, that would probably have been enough to switch twenty-five thousand votes and reëlect him. Senator Tydings also went down to defeat in November, and he believed that he lost because of his general support for the civil-rights cause, which, of course, included his vote against Carswell.

Senator Fulbright was also in difficulty at home for his vote against Carswell, but since he wasn't up for reëlection until 1974, and rumor had it that he meant to retire then, he didn't need any help from the Administration. He got it anyway. At two o'clock on the morning following the vote, Attorney General Mitchell's wife telephoned the *Arkansas Gazette*, said, "I'm little Martha Mitchell," rambled on for a few minutes about her childhood in Arkansas, described how enraged she was by Carswell's defeat, and added, "I want you to crucify Fulbright, and that's it." The *Gazette*, which had opposed Carswell from the start, printed an account of her call on the front page of the next edition, and Fulbright's stock soared in Arkansas.

A couple of weeks after the vote, a senator from the Deep South who confessed to having some admiration for the idea of the Southern strategy cited the Administration's failure to implement it by way of the Haynsworth and Carswell nominations to prove that it would never succeed. "Mr. Nixon has no feeling for, and no understanding of, the South," he said shortly after Carswell was defeated. "One of the things he doesn't understand is that among Southerners' many antediluvian attitudes is the attitude of fierce independence."

Several other senators, from both the South and the North,

felt that the President had so misunderstood the Senate's own sense of independence in the Carswell fight that he had made it far fiercer than it would normally have been. One of the most immediate and direct results turned up a couple of weeks later when he announced the invasion of Cambodia, which produced an unprecedented reaction in the Senate. "The President forced us to face our responsibilities and assert our rights in the Carswell affair," one Republican senator remarked at the time. "Without that renewed sense of our authority, it is extremely doubtful that so many senators would have stood up to him on Cambodia. While they lost on that in the end, he lost even more—the longstanding bipartisan support on international crises." When the lawyers and students poured into the capital by the thousands to protest the Cambodia invasion, they repeatedly cited the results of the Carswell vote to demonstrate their strength. Unaware of their determination, Mr. Nixon had involved them in politics in a way that their friends in Washington never could have.

Carswell's announcement that he was resigning from the bench to run for the Senate in Florida led even some of his staunchest defenders to conclude that his enemies had been right in charging that he was more politician than judge and lacked the temperament to serve on any high court. That his sponsor was the governor of Florida, Claude Kirk, a flagrant white-supremacist, also convinced many of them that the racial charges against Carswell were true. In addition, some senators were puzzled by his desire to join a club that had already blackballed him. After his stunning defeat in the primary—by nearly two to one—Carswell apparently retired from public life. He was obviously an embittered man.

But no one was as embittered as the President who had nominated him. Immediately after the vote, all the White

House press office would say about the President's reaction was that "he, of course, was disappointed." How disappointed he was emerged the following day, after he had spent an evening cruising on the Potomac in the Presidential yacht *Sequoia* with Attorney General Mitchell. Summoning the White House press corps the next morning, Mr. Nixon, with the Attorney General at his side, delivered a bitter tirade against the Senate. "I have reluctantly concluded—with the Senate presently constituted—I cannot successfully nominate to the Supreme Court any federal appellate judge from the South who believes as I do in the strict construction of the Constitution," he began. Going on to charge that the vote had been the result of "vicious assaults," "malicious character assassination," and an "act of regional discrimination," he wound up by saying that he would be compelled to find his next nominee in the North.

Many people felt that this was merely a political statement, but one prominent lawyer who was deeply involved in the Carswell fight said, "He meant it. Those of us who raised our heads out of the trenches in this fight will never be forgiven. As far as the President is concerned, anyone who was against him on this one is just plain against him."

In the Senate, the reaction to the President's remarks ranged from outrage to disbelief to amusement. Republicans, by and large, were the angriest—with good reason, as Bayh saw it. "These senators felt that the President had handed them two lemons, had gone to the mat for his choices when he didn't have to, and then had attacked the Senate for doing its job," he said. Schweiker was particularly distressed by the President's attack, and called it "a total misreading of the mood, the temper, and the meaning of what the debate was about." Brooke found it "incredible that the President would make such a mistaken and unfortunate statement." And Tydings rose on the Senate floor and ticked off a list of federal judges in the South whom he and just about everybody else would have been happy to confirm.

When tempers had subsided a little, a senator who had worked and voted for Carswell—John Sherman Cooper, the Senate's most courtly member—attempted to put the furious charges and countercharges into perspective. "That's all part of the way we do business here," he said with a smile. "It's just politics. I don't see how the attacks have hurt anybody. Whatever I may personally feel about the outcome, I'm sure the debate showed the people, including the people in Congress, what the Supreme Court should be and what the Senate could be."

INDEX

THE AUTHOR

Richard Harris is the author of JUSTICE: *The Crisis of Law, Order, and Freedom in America,* called by *The New York Times* "a basic sourcebook to studies of the sixties and after." Mr. Harris, a staff writer for *The New Yorker* magazine for the past fifteen years, has written widely on the subject of politics in America. His previous books include *The Real Voice, A Sacred Trust,* and *The Fear of Crime.*